The
Psychic
Bible

The
Psychic
Bible

THE DEFINITIVE GUIDE
TO DEVELOPING YOUR
PSYCHIC SKILLS

Jane Struthers

STERLING
New York / London
www.sterlingpublishing.com

Library of Congress Cataloging in Publication
Data Available

2   4   6   8   10   9   7   5   3   1

Published in 2007 by Sterling Publishing Co., Inc.
387 Park Avenue South, New York, NY 10016

Copyright © Octopus Publishing Group Ltd 2007
Text copyright © Jane Struthers 2007

First published in Great Britain in 2007 by Godsfield
A division of Octopus Publishing Group Ltd
2–4 Heron Quays, London E14 4JP, England

Distributed in Canada by Sterling Publishing
c/o Canadian Manda Group, 165 Dufferin Street,
Toronto, Ontario, Canada M6K 3H6

For information about custom editions, special sales,
premium and corporate purchases, please contact
Sterling Special Sales Department at 800-805-5489
or specialsales@sterlingpub.com.

Manufactured in China

Sterling ISBN-13: 978-1-4027-5226-1
Sterling ISBN-10: 1-4027-5226-1

Contents

Introduction

Defining psychic powers

If you have ever used your sixth sense, you have used your psychic powers. As humans, most of us have five physical senses that we frequently take for granted: sight, hearing, smell, taste and touch. We are so used to them that we don't always notice how much we depend on them. But we are less confident about using our so-called sixth sense, or psychic ability. For a start, it can be very difficult to define this, because we can't see it, smell it or touch it: it is subtle and invisible. We might experience it as a strange feeling in the pit of our stomach or as a sudden knowledge for which we can't give a logical explanation. We simply know that we've tuned into something mysterious, nebulous or even rather eerie.

Psychic powers cover a wide range of abilities. You could think of them as a switch: some people are born with this switch fully activated, so that even as children they are completely connected to their sixth sense or psychic ability; other people have to work hard to activate their psychic ability, rather as they would if they wanted to learn to play a musical instrument. They find that, with practice, what seemed to them at first such a foreign activity gradually becomes second nature. And some people never consciously connect with their psychic abilities, perhaps because they're frightened of them or think they are sent from the devil; alternatively, they don't believe in such

Being psychic means being tuned in to an unseen world of sensations and ideas.

things because science can't explain them. Well, not yet, anyway.

People who are very psychic are tuned into a world that is invisible to their non-psychic companions. They may be able to see ghosts and spirits, tune into atmospheres, see auras or know things about other people without being told. However, psychic ability need not be quite so dramatic, and it may come and go for no apparent reason.

With practice you'll discover which psychic tools work most effectively for you.

How this book can help you

Whether your own psychic switch is already set to "on" or whether you're at the start of your journey into developing your psychic senses, this book will help you to develop your psychic skills. It will lead you through a variety of techniques, including working with your body's subtle energy system, energy healing, giving yourself psychic protection and contacting your spirit guides. The directory of psychic skills at the back of the book will help you take things one step further.

Different psychic powers

When you first start to develop your psychic powers you may not be able to slot them into a particular category. You might have the knack of knowing who is on the phone simply by listening to its tone when it rings. Maybe you sometimes know things about another person without having to be told. Or perhaps you enjoy visiting old buildings because you get such a strong sense of the people who used to live there. You may not even think much of such gifts, because you have had them throughout your life. Yet these are all examples of psychic ability, and they all have a particular name.

Crystal balls come in many shapes and sizes, but it's important to use the one that suits you best.

As you practice and gain in confidence, your readings will become richer and more intuitive.

The four types of psychic ability

Psychic abilities can be divided into four categories. Most people who want to develop their psychic talents find that they have a natural bent towards any two of the categories, such as being clairvoyant and claircognizant. None of the categories is better or more spiritually evolved than any other, so there is no pecking order involved.

Clairvoyance

This is the psychic ability with which most of us are familiar. Clairvoyance means "clear seeing," and it describes the ability to see spirit forms. These appear either as a materialization or in the mind's eye.

Clairaudience

When someone is clairaudient, it means she has the gift of clear hearing. She can hear spirit voices and noises, either inside her head or as external sounds.

Clairsentience

Clairsentience means "clear feeling." This might be experienced as the ability to tune into the atmosphere in a room or to experience other people's emotional or physical distress as though it were happening to the clairsentient himself. Hunches and other forms of intuition also come into the category of clairsentience.

Claircognizance

This is the least well known of the four psychic talents. It means "clear knowing," and describes the ability to know things without being told and to receive fully formed ideas.

How is psychic ability possible?

At first glance we all seem to be separate from each other. I am separate from you, and you are separate from your neighbor. We imagine that we are all separate entities who connect with each other purely by choice. But are we?

Mystics have believed for millennia that we are all connected. The Buddha spoke of this, and so did Jesus Christ. So, instead of us all being separate little worlds that orbit one another and connect only when we wish to, from a mystical point of view I am you and you are your neighbor. You are even your neighbor's cat. And your neighbor's cat is you. There is no difference between us.

THE SCIENTIFIC EXPLANATION

What is so interesting about this is that science, having poured scorn on such ideas (and especially on religious concepts) for centuries, is finally starting to agree. Science is now discovering what many psychics have known for a long time—that we are all linked by our energy fields. There are different terms for these energy fields and you will find different explanations of them, too, because we are still in the early stages of understanding them. For instance, Dr. Rupert Sheldrake, a

Scientists are starting to explore the energy fields that surround us all.

British scientist who researches animal behavior among other things, refers to these energy fields as "morphic resonance."

It is beyond the scope of this book to explore the science of energy fields in great detail. And you could argue that anyone who needs to be given a scientific explanation for his psychic abilities is looking at the equation from the wrong perspective. Someone who is psychic doesn't need science to validate his experiences before he can believe in them or place his faith in them.

IN THE LABORATORY

If science is starting to grasp the concept that everything is linked to everything else through energy fields, does that mean that science can now observe those energy fields in action? In some cases, yes. For instance, Kirlian photography can capture the aura (the subtle-energy system, see pages 82–83) of a living entity on camera. But very often scientific methods are not suited to the testing of psychic abilities. Science has to test a phenomenon repeatedly in order to understand it. And while a camera can take endless

Kirlian photography reveals the aura of any living entity. It clearly shows points of energy around the edge of this leaf.

photographs of the auras of leaves, people and animals, humans are not able to repeat experiments in the same way. By definition, psychic people are sensitive and may react adversely when pressured to perform in a laboratory. This is probably why mediums and other psychics can provide utterly convincing proof of their talents in their consulting rooms, but experience a dramatic decline in their success rate when asked to give readings under scientific conditions. To complicate matters, it has been found, even in non-scientific conditions, that repeating a psychic test several times leads to a severely diminished success rate.

Nevertheless, some psychics have been able to cope with laboratory tests, with astonishing results. In the early 1970s Uri Geller participated in extensive tests at various laboratories around the world. At Stanford Research Institute (now called SRI International) in California, he took part in (and succeeded at) a great many experiments, including one in which he influenced a gram weight that was sitting under a bell jar, by making it weigh less and then weigh more.

MAKING UP YOUR OWN MIND

The best way to assess the evidence for and against psychic phenomena, and to gain some understanding of how it works, is to experience it yourself. If you have never been for a reading with a medium or never received psychic healing, perhaps it is time to start. Alternatively, if you'd like to experiment with your own psychic powers, but are unsure how to begin, you could simply start by writing down every intuition, hunch, premonition and so-called coincidence that you experience. You might discover that you are tapping into something bigger than yourself. Pay more attention to your psychic abilities and they will start to develop.

Zener cards are one of the classic ways of testing someone's telepathic powers.

Is everyone psychic?

Not everyone is born with all five of their physical senses intact. Babies can be born blind, deaf or with any other physical problem that will compromise or affect one of their senses. But every child is born with some level of psychic ability. It is what he does with it that is the real crux of the matter.

PSYCHIC CHILDREN

Small children regularly use their natural psychic abilities. Many children have invisible playmates when they're young. Are these friends merely figments of

Psychic ability starts at birth, although it's up to each of us what we do with it.

Small children often demonstrate a remarkable and instinctive psychic ability.

Children use their psychic talents in many different ways, and they believe in them. But they usually stop doing so at about the age of seven, when they start to take more notice of the well-meaning adults around them who reprimand them for making up stories. For instance, they may be told that they're too old now to have invisible playmates or to pretend that there's the ghost of an old man in the spare bedroom. They learn to keep quiet about their psychic experiences because these get them into trouble, and very often their psychic powers start to wane, partly from lack of use and partly from a diminishing belief in them.

their over-active imaginations or can the children genuinely see these companions? In fact, children often report being visited by people who, when they are described, turn out to be deceased members of the family, such as their grandparents. Many children can also remember fragments of their past lives, although this ability usually wanes over time. As you might expect, there is a higher incidence of children who can recall their past lives in cultures where reincarnation is an accepted belief.

PSYCHIC ADULTS

If you recognize yourself in these descriptions, don't despair because you can easily reactivate your psychic abilities. Even if you weren't psychic as a child, you can still awaken your dormant psychic gifts. Because the answer to the question "Is everyone psychic?" is: yes, to some degree everyone is. We all have some level of natural psychic ability, and we can all develop it further if we wish to do so.

Is it just my imagination?

When you start to tap into your psychic abilities, it can be very difficult to know whether you are actually using your powers or simply imagining that they are working. They normally manifest in very subtle ways, so it can be hard to tell what's going on at first.

A crystal pendulum is a very sensitive instrument in the right hands.

After all, if psychic powers announced themselves with a great fanfare, or we could all perform telekinesis and move objects around a room at will, science would long ago have accepted the existence of such abilities.

Deciding whether your psychic powers are simply a result of your imagination is very important. You want to know whether you're receiving genuine psychic input or whether something else is happening. There are two ways to do this. The first is to ensure that you are calm and centerd before starting to use your psychic powers, and the second is to keep an open mind and remain positive.

STAY CALM

If you don't feel balanced and calm, you won't be able to detect any changes in your energy field, or aura, when they happen. These changes tell you that you have made a psychic connection with something. But you won't notice them if you're feeling tense and edgy.

KEEP AN OPEN MIND

If you don't keep an open mind about your psychic experiments, you will either interpret every event as having a psychic message for you, or you will tell yourself that you are wasting your time and nothing is happening. Neither attitude is helpful because it comes from a closed mind. If you believe that every little shiver or sensation you experience indicates a psychic connection, you're being just as

Meditation is an excellent way to put yourself in a calm state of mind.

dogmatic as if you tell yourself there is no such thing as psychic ability. Even experienced mediums stay open to the idea that an apparent communication from a spirit might be nothing more than their imagination working overtime. That is why they always ask the spirit for evidence before believing that they've made contact.

Are psychic powers dangerous?

Horror films and books have a lot to answer for. They often tell the story of someone who starts off completely innocent and usually slightly naïve, then begins to develop her psychic powers and in doing so unleashes a torrent of evil forces that destroy the lives of everyone around her. Reality is somewhat different.

TAKE SIMPLE PRECAUTIONS

Yes, there may be dangers in developing your psychic powers, but these problems only arise if you fail to protect yourself properly. Even this idea can sound rather alarming, but in fact it is perfectly sensible and reasonable. Would you leave your front door wide open day and night, so that anyone—friend or foe—could wander off the street into your house? No. Would you contact a complete stranger, about whom you knew nothing, and invite him to spend a day with you or let him influence all your thoughts and actions? No. If you got chatting to a stranger on

the bus and she began to tell you what you should be doing with your life, would you follow her advice without questioning it? Probably not. You might even get off the bus early so that you could get away from her.

Yet despite being careful to lock their doors to keep out unwelcome intruders, some people willingly allow members of the spirit world to have complete, unrestricted access to them without checking their credentials first. There are some simple ways to do this, as you will soon discover. You must "test the spirits," as St. Paul put it, by asking them if they come with good intentions. If you start to develop your psychic powers without knowing what you are dealing with, your life may not end up being a mirror of Stephen King's classic horror novel *Carrie*, but you could still have some unpleasant and unnerving experiences.

It really is far better to be safe than sorry. Don't worry about offending the spirits by asking them if they are benign. They will expect you to do so.

If you join a psychic circle, make sure it's led by someone who knows what he's doing.

Ways to prepare yourself

Before you begin to make a conscious effort to develop your psychic powers, you must prepare yourself. If you do this, you will be able to strengthen the connection you make with your intuition and with any spirits or guides you might contact, and you will also have a much better idea of when your psychic abilities are being activated.

If you don't make any preparations for your psychic work, you will never get very far and you won't know whether the impressions you are receiving come from your own mind or from outside influences.

It is very important to ground and balance yourself before you begin any psychic work, and you will find the exercise in this section (see pages 24–25). But you can do other things as well to prepare yourself.

Remaining calm and balanced helps you to tune into your psychic abilities.

RITUALS

One highly effective way to prepare yourself for psychic work is to perform a ritual. This can be as simple or as complicated as you like; it may be nothing more elaborate than lighting a candle, holding a crystal, chanting "Om" or playing a specific piece of music. Do whatever feels comfortable and puts you in a suitable frame of mind. For instance, when choosing music you will get better results if you play a soothing piece of classical or sacred music than if you opt for a raucous rock song. You want to be relaxed and contemplative, not buzzing with adrenalin and ready for a rip-roaring party.

CANDLES

If you decide to light some candles, choose their color carefully. Ideally you should use white candles, as these send out a purifying and protective energy. You can use either tall candles or votives, but always make sure you use them safely to avoid any possibility of accidentally starting a fire. Avoid red or black candles, which send out very powerful energies that are inappropriate for this sort of work.

It can be very helpful to carry out a special ritual before beginning your psychic work.

Grounding and balancing yourself

The first step when preparing yourself to tune into your psychic powers is always to ground and balance yourself. If you feel centered within yourself and in a calm frame of mind, then you will find it easier to detect any changes in your emotions or your physical body, which could be coming from your psychic powers. For example, if you're already feeling anxious and nervous, you won't know if any additional feelings are coming from inside you or from external forces. If your mind is already teeming with thoughts, you won't notice if any additional ideas occur to you.

Although the grounding exercise on the opposite page should always be used before you perform any psychic work, it is also excellent whenever you feel unsettled or anxious. As you become more comfortable with the exercise you will be able to perform it anywhere, even when standing in line at your local supermarket. Try to make this exercise part of your daily routine.

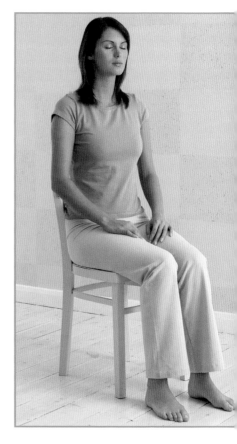

GROUNDING EXERCISE

When you initially do this exercise it will seem to take a long time, but it will become easier, and quicker, with practice. At first you should conduct the exercise sitting down, but later on you will be able to do it standing up, if you wish.

1 Sit comfortably in a chair, with both feet flat on the floor. If your feet don't reach the floor, place a cushion beneath them. If it is physically impossible for you to place your feet on the floor, do so in your imagination instead.

2 Take three deep breaths, releasing any tension that you feel on each out-breath, then breathe normally.

3 Imagine that roots are growing out of the soles of your feet down into the ground. It helps to imagine that your feet are enormous, so that you can create more roots. Hear or see these roots penetrating deep into the earth's crust, down into the center of the planet. Know that they are growing and multiplying, and in doing so are connecting you to the energy and solidity of the earth.

4 Now imagine that energy from the earth is being sent up the roots into your feet and is filling your entire body with white light. You might like to imagine that the energy flows in with each in-breath until your entire body is suffused with light.

Synchronicity and coincidence

When is a coincidence not a coincidence? When it's an example of synchronicity. This is a concept that was developed by Carl Jung, the famous Swiss psychoanalyst, and Wolfgang Pauli, a Swiss physicist. Synchronicity means "a coincidence in time," but Jung used it specifically to describe what he called "an acausal connecting theory" that creates a meaningful relationship between two events that take place at the same time.

THE FLOCK OF BIRDS

How does synchronicity work in reality? The classic example that pointed Jung in the direction of synchronicity involved one of his patients. This man's wife had told Jung that, when both her mother and grandmother died, many birds gathered outside the room in which they were dying. Jung's patient was ill with what Jung suspected was heart disease, and the patient was referred to a heart specialist. On his way home from being given a clean bill of health by the specialist, he collapsed in the street. When his body was brought home, it was greeted by his wife, who already suspected that something awful had happened to her husband because a flock of birds had gathered on their house while he was out.

WHAT DOES THIS TELL US?

You could argue that the flock of birds is merely a coincidence, but it is certainly a remarkable one and it definitely had a special meaning for the patient's wife. You could also argue that flocks of birds might have gathered on the woman's house at other times that didn't coincide with the death of a close family member. However, that is not the point. The fact is that the birds congregated during the deaths of the mother, grandmother and husband, and the woman believed there was a meaning in these events.

There are no rules about what constitutes synchronicity. It's entirely personal.

How psychic am I?

If you're reading this book, you are probably already interested in psychic phenomena and want to know how to introduce more psychic experiences into your life. You may also be wondering about how much psychic power you already have.

Answer the following questions as honestly as you can, with either a "Yes" or a "No." Even if you suspect that you aren't very psychic, that may not be true. There are many cases of people whose psychic powers developed relatively late, often with extraordinary results that changed their lives.

Do your best to remain open to the idea that you can become more psychic than you are at the moment. This will encourage your unconscious mind to pick up more psychic phenomena. If, on the other hand, you tell yourself that you aren't psychic, and never will be, you will dramatically reduce the power of your psychic abilities.

☐ Have you ever had a premonition that worked out exactly as you'd predicted?

☐ When you were a child, did you have companions that only you could see?

☐ Have you ever seen or sensed a ghost?

☐ Have you ever felt unable to enter a room or building because you couldn't bear its unpleasant atmosphere?

☐ Have any of your dreams ever come true?

Past experiences

☐ Have you ever correctly sensed that a loved one was in danger?

☐ Have you ever thought about someone and then immediately received a phone call from them?

☐ Have you ever seen fuzzy lights around animate or inanimate objects?

☐ Have you ever noticed strong smells, which might have had a special significance for you, that no one else could detect?

☐ Have you ever had a "peak experience," in which you felt there was no division between you and the world around you?

☐ Have you ever decided not to buy something because you didn't like the atmosphere emanating from it?

☐ Have you ever touched an object and been swamped by sensations or emotions that didn't belong to you?

☐ Have you ever felt depressed or tearful for no apparent reason, then heard about a major disaster soon afterwards?

Present experiences

☐ Do you sometimes know who's on the other end of the phone before you pick it up?

☐ Do you have a special affinity with animals?

☐ Do you instinctively know, without being told, when someone is feeling ill?

☐ Do you have an adverse effect on machines, such as computers, when you're angry or upset?

☐ Do people tell you that you're too sensitive and easily hurt?

☐ Do you believe in the power of the mind over the body?

☐ Do you sometimes know what someone is going to say even before they've opened their mouth?

☐ Do the palms of your hands ever tingle when you're with people who are ill?

☐ Do you see things out of the corner of your eye that aren't there when you look again?

☐ Do you trust your hunches, especially when investing money?

☐ When you're expecting visitors do you usually sense their arrival before you can see or hear them?

☐ Do you believe in angels and fairies, even if you have never seen one of them?

Adding up your score

Now count up the number of times you answered "Yes" to a question, then look up your score below.

25–19 You have strong psychic abilities that can be developed. You might be interested in joining a psychic development circle.

18–12 You may be a lot more psychic than you realize. Allow your thoughts and impressions to flow.

11–6 Keep up the good work! Your innate psychic abilities are waiting to be developed further.

5–0 Don't give up hope. You may be blocking some of your psychic impressions for some reason, such as fear. Practice being more open–minded.

Don't expect your innate psychic abilities to develop overnight. They may take time.

Exploring the mind

How the mind works

The human mind is a mystery. Many eminent psychologists have attempted to explain it, but no one has yet done so categorically because it doesn't have a physical location and therefore can't be examined. The mind may be contained within the brain or it may be located outside the body: some people argue that the mind is really the spirit and that it has no specific location with the human body; when that body dies, the mind or spirit departs and leaves only a fleshy shell.

Scans can reveal different areas of brain activity.

BRAIN VERSUS MIND

Our brains regulate our physical behavior and the many complex systems within our bodies, including the autonomic nervous system, which controls all our unconscious bodily functions. Our minds, on the other hand, do none of these things, as far as we know. You might like to think of them as the parts of our brains that give us our individual personalities, complete with a whole host of idiosyncrasies and quirks. It is probably our minds, rather than our brains, that generate psychic ability such as telepathy and precognition.

THE FREUDIAN APPROACH

The function of the mind has fascinated many great psychiatrists and psychotherapists, including Carl Jung and Sigmund Freud. They all developed their own systems for explaining how the mind works and what makes us uniquely human. Jung's ideas are

Sigmund Freud divided the human mind into five compartments: the Ego, the Id, the Superego, the conscious and the subconscious.

explained in greater depth later in this section (see pages 46–49).

For Freud, who was the founder of psychoanalysis, our human personalities are influenced by our unconscious minds. The very fact that this part of our minds is unconscious means that we're unaware of it, and therefore unaware of the way it affects us. Freud believed that our unconscious minds are particularly influenced by our hidden conflicts, which arise from the trauma of our sexual experiences in childhood. We repress our unpleasant sexual memories in the hope that they'll go away, but they disappear into the unconscious, where they reappear as neurotic behavior. They also reappear in our dreams, which Freud believed could be analyzed in order to unpick and treat our neuroses.

Altered states of consciousness

The five wavebands

- **Delta waves** operate at the slowest rate and occur during deep sleep.
- **Theta waves** occur naturally during sleep. They are also connected with creativity, intuition and trance-like states.
- **Alpha waves** are dominant early in the morning and when we're relaxed. They are connected with the creative process.
- **Beta waves** occur when we're busy and active. They hamper the creative process.
- **Gamma waves** are the fastest of all and are associated with complex thinking.

At first glance we might appear to have two states of consciousness—awake and asleep. In fact, our brains are much more complicated than that. Scientists currently believe that our brain activity is divided into five wavebands: delta, theta, alpha, beta and gamma.

SHAMANISTIC TRADITIONS

Many cultures deliberately induce theta and alpha brain waves in order to enter altered states of consciousness.

Shamans, for example, do this through such activities as ritualistic drumming, chanting and dancing. Entering a different level of consciousness enables them to perform healing and divination.

BRAIN WAVES AND CREATIVITY

We are at our most creative when our brains are in an alpha or theta state. Coffee and other stimulants wake us up and interfere with these brain waves, whereas we are much more creative when we're feeling relaxed. There are some remarkable instances of drowsy states being linked to creativity. When Elias Howe was struggling to invent a needle for his prototype sewing machine, he dreamed that a tribal king ordered him to create a sewing machine. When he said that he couldn't, the entire tribe banged their spears repeatedly on the ground. Howe realized that there was a hole just below the point of each spear, and that the spears looked and moved like sewing needles. This knowledge enabled him to manufacture an efficient sewing machine.

Opposite page: Rhythmic drumming is a good way to induce an alpha state.

When we want to solve a problem we often say that we'll "sleep on it."

Leaving the body

Normally we are firmly tethered in our bodies. We may be so used to this situation that we don't even think about it. However, occasionally something can happen that makes us temporarily leave our bodies.

THE ASTRAL BODY

Humans have believed in the existence of the astral body for centuries. It is thought to be an exact replica of the physical body, to which it is joined by a silver cord. Usually the astral and physical bodies are perfectly aligned, but sometimes (for various reasons) they can become separated. It is when this happens that we have the sensation of leaving our bodies.

OUT–OF–BODY EXPERIENCES

These are also known as OOBEs and can occur spontaneously. People who have experienced such OOBEs report being in their bodies one moment and then suddenly finding themselves outside their bodies. They might be floating above their bodies and able to see them, or they might find themselves in completely different and alien surroundings, such as whirling through space. After the experience is over, the person having the OOBE reports the sensation of reentering their body, often through their head. They variously describe this as easy or difficult.

OOBEs are believed to involve the person's astral body temporarily leaving the confines of the physical body. Very often the person describes being able to see the silver cord linking his astral body to his physical body, and being aware that he will die if this silver cord is severed.

Sometimes a person will have an OOBE during an operation or while he is ill. However, he is equally likely to have one while he is asleep or before he falls asleep, when he is perfectly well.

Out-of-body experiences are believed to be examples of astral travel.

Many people who have had near-death experiences (NDEs) speak of going through a tunnel.

NEAR-DEATH EXPERIENCES

There is nothing new about near-death experiences (NDEs), which were recorded in the *Tibetan Book of the Dead* from the 8th century BCE. Once called death-bed visions, NDEs are now the subject of books and lengthy studies to determine whether they really exist. What is striking about them is that they all conform to more or less the same pattern. Perhaps most remarkable of all is that people who have NDEs are changed for ever by the experience. They may become more sensitive or compassionate as a result; they may make dramatic changes to their lives; or they may discover hidden talents.

As its name implies, an NDE occurs when someone is on the brink of death. She spontaneously leaves her body and at first is aware of everything that is going on around her. She floats towards a dark tunnel, which she enters, and emerges into bright light where she is greeted by friendly people, who may be deceased loved ones, strangers or religious figures such as angels or Jesus Christ. She then has a review of her life, in which she assesses what she has learned and what she still needs to learn. It is usually at this point that she is told she must return to Earth, and reluctantly reenters her body.

Sceptics claim that NDEs are nothing more than the sensations that are experienced while the brain dies, but they are unable to explain why people who have these experiences are frequently able to describe in complete detail what has been going on around them during the NDE. In some cases people describe what they saw on top of wardrobes or cupboards when they floated up to the ceiling, and hospital patients can recount events that took place in other parts of the building during their NDEs.

ASTRAL PROJECTION

Some people claim to be able to leave their bodies at will and travel on the astral plane. They can then visit other places or watch people they know, while remaining invisible themselves, before returning to their bodies. This is a very similar process to an OOBE. Astral projection is sometimes confused with etheric projection, in which the person leaves his body, but is clearly seen by whoever he visits.

Tapping into states of consciousness

Long before scientists were able to measure and record brain waves (see pages 36–37), humans knew how to enter different states of consciousness. They did this by eating and drinking hallucinogenic substances, such as the peyote cactus, as well as by engaging in rituals that were designed to throw them out of their normal world into something more mystical or supernatural. However, we can enter these states of consciousness without resorting to drugs. Meditation, chanting, yoga and fasting are all ways to do this.

We are relaxed and creative whenever our brains are emitting alpha waves. This state occurs naturally first thing in the morning, just after waking, so it makes sense to exploit it by setting aside this section of the day for meditation or a creative activity. In monastic societies, both in the West and East, monks and nuns rise early to spend time in prayer and meditation. Many writers take advantage of the creativity of their natural alpha states by getting up early in order to work.

You can meditate cross-legged on the floor or on a chair if that's more comfortable for you.

INDUCING AN ALPHA STATE

If you want to improve your psychic abilities, you may find that your intuition works especially well first thing in the morning, while you are still feeling slightly sleepy. However, you can induce an alpha state at any time of the day.

1 Whenever you want to promote an alpha state, relax your body as much as possible and close your eyes.

2 Place the tip of your tongue against the back of your two top front teeth, at the point where they meet the bony ridge below your soft palate. Hold your tongue there for as long as you wish your alpha state to continue. You can experiment by doing this when you're writing something creative, meditating, giving healing, practicing yoga or using your psychic abilities.

MEDITATION

Meditation fulfils many functions. It's an excellent way to relax, so it has a beneficial impact on our health and can even help in reducing blood-pressure levels and general anxiety. Meditation is a very good method of clearing the mind, to give us sharper focus and greater clarity of thought. It can also help to increase our psychic abilities by enabling us to make contact with the spirit realms.

One of the beauties of meditation is that you don't need any special equipment. You can meditate while sitting cross-legged on the floor, with a cushion to support the base of your spine, or sitting in a chair or on a Zen bench (which supports you while you kneel on the floor). What is important is to be comfortable, because you won't be able to focus on your meditation if your back aches or your legs have gone to sleep.

This man is sitting in the half-lotus position, but it isn't a prerequisite for meditation.

Different forms of meditation

There are many different ways to meditate. You might like to experiment until you find the method that suits you best, or you may prefer to develop a variety of techniques. Whenever you're bothered by unwanted thoughts, acknowledge them without getting caught up in them—let them go. It may help to picture these thoughts as clouds, and to imagine them wafting away from you each time they arise. At first, you should aim to meditate for about 20 minutes twice a week. Build up the number of sessions gradually, to give yourself time to get used to them. Here are some suggestions for different meditations.

• **Focused meditation**, on an object, such as a candle flame or a crystal.

• **Visualization meditation**, in which you imagine going on a journey or meeting a spirit guide.

• **Guided meditation**, in which you listen to a pre-recorded tape or CD of a meditation.

• **Transcendental meditation** (TM), in which you continually repeat a mantra.

• **Listening meditation**, in which you keep your eyes open and listen to what is happening around you. The aim is to remain alert and aware of your surroundings.

• **Buddhist meditation**, in which you observe the inhalation and exhalation of the breath.

The legacy of Carl Jung

The work of Carl Jung has exerted a formidable influence over Western thinking since the early 20th century. Born in Switzerland in 1875, Jung trained as a psychiatrist. From the outset of his career he was fascinated by the occult, embracing and exploring it in a way that eventually put him at odds with his mentor, Sigmund Freud, who regarded it as a "black tide of mud." Freud and Jung also eventually differed in opinion about the influence of sexual repression on our personalities (Jung disagreed with Freud about its importance), and eventually they realized that they could no longer work together.

THE COLLECTIVE UNCONSCIOUS

Jung was fascinated by dreams and always paid attention to his own. Unlike Freud, who viewed the unconscious (or subconscious, as he preferred to call it) as a dumping ground for all the things connected with our past that we don't like to think about, Jung saw the unconscious as a rich repository of ideas and symbols from every culture, and believed that it tells us about our future as well as our past.

He crystallized his theories about the unconscious in 1909 after he had what is now a famous dream, about being on the first floor of an old house. It was well-furnished, but he realized he didn't know what the lower floor was like, so he went to look. Here, everything was much older and darker. Jung saw a trapdoor in the floor, which led him down to a cave littered with broken pottery and bones, including two ancient human skulls.

When analyzing the dream, Jung realized that it represented the psyche, or mind. The top floor was his conscious personality. The lower floor was the first level of the unconscious, which Jung dubbed the personal unconscious. The cave represented the primitive part of Jung's psyche, which he called "a world which can scarcely be reached or illuminated by

During his life, Carl Jung was fascinated by such topics as alchemy, astrology, folklore and mythology.

consciousness." He termed this the "collective unconscious," because it is common to all humans.

JUNG AND THE OCCULT

Jung investigated many branches of the occult. He trained himself to read astrological charts and became fascinated by the I Ching (see pages 200–207). He considered both astrology and the I Ching to be prime examples of synchronicity (see pages 26–27). Jung was introduced to the I Ching when he met Richard Wilhelm, the celebrated German author of a book about the I Ching. When this book was translated into English, Jung wrote the introduction.

Mandalas

Jung's receptivity to the images and symbols of other cultures led him in many directions. During World War I, while he was the commandant of a camp for British internees, he began to draw circular patterns that he quickly realized were mandalas ("mandala" is Sanskrit for circle). Each mandala represented his psychic state on the day he drew it, and he found the entire process immensely helpful. It enabled him to gather together the strands of his life and find a point of focus within them.

Mandalas date back to ancient times and have been found all over the world in many different cultures, including the American southwest. They are usually circular, but very often also contain some form of quadrant, such as a square, cross or a triangle.

For instance, a mandala might be divided into quadrants that mirror each other and are decorated in harmonious patterns. Jung believed that mandalas hold extraordinary power because they are sacred images that represent the integrated psyche—the goal for which we are all striving.

When working with a mandala, you can draw your own in exactly the same way as Jung, or you can study one that has already been created. Many cathedrals, such as Chartres and Notre-Dame in France, contain circular stained-glass windows that are mandalas. In Tibetan culture, beautifully intricate mandalas are often created with colored sand, studied for a while and then swept away, ready for new versions to take their place.

Dreams

Dreams provide a fascinating insight into the workings of our unconscious minds.

Everyone dreams. Dreaming is an essential part of our mental health, for reasons that science is still exploring. If we go without sleep for even a few days, we run the risk of becoming psychotic —a condition that can cause irreversible brain damage. After even one night without sleep, we will start to hallucinate while we're awake, or take brief catnaps in which we have vivid dreams. These are both ways for our brains to catch up with our essential dreaming, in order to keep ourselves healthy. When we get a proper night's sleep again, we will have a string of vivid dreams.

WHAT ARE DREAMS?

Although we might be asleep for eight hours at a time, we don't dream for that entire period. Instead, we have periodic sessions of dreaming, during which we experience rapid eye movements (REM). At the end of the dream, we return to a dreamless state before the next session of REM begins.

Our age determines the amount of time we spend dreaming. Babies dream most of all, and people who are senile are thought to dream the least. Animals dream, too.

A DREAM'S MESSAGE

Some people think that dreams are nothing more than our brains emptying themselves of redundant information. But psychotherapy places tremendous importance on our dreams, believing that they shed light on our unconscious minds and that, as a result, they carry important messages for us. Analyzing our dreams is a way for us to understand our unconscious and come to terms with problems that are bothering us.

ASTRAL TRAVEL

Do we stay in our bodies while we're asleep or do we go traveling on the astral planes? Many people believe that we do indeed have astral journeys when we're asleep, and this would certainly explain the very vivid dreams that we can have, in which we encounter people who have died or find ourselves in ethereal surroundings. It is a common experience to dream that we are being taught important information, even though we may not remember it when we wake up; it is still stored in our unconscious minds. There are also theories that when we dream of flying through the sky like a bird—a relatively common experience—we are actually on an astral journey.

PRECOGNITIVE DREAMS

Sometimes dreams have an apparently uncanny way of coming true. These are called precognitive dreams and there are many recorded instances of them, including those in the archives first created by Dr. J. B. Rhine at Duke University in North Carolina in the 1930s. His daughter, Sally Rhine Feather, is still adding to the collection. People who report their precognitive dreams usually describe the precise way in which those dreams are played out in reality. Even tiny details from the dreams can be replicated when the event takes place.

It seems that most precognitive dreams involve unpleasant incidents, such as seeing a loved one in pain or dreaming that someone will die. It may be that we have precognitive dreams about happy experiences too, but perhaps we don't pay as much attention to them as we do to unsettling dreams, which have a greater ability to stay with us. Sometimes a dream seems to make little sense at the time and it is only later that we realize it was a premonition. For instance, many people around the world experienced strange dreams as well as waking hallucinations about seeing flames and smoke coming out of tall buildings before the attacks on the World Trade Center and the Pentagon on September 11, 2001. It was only after these attacks took place that the full significance of the precognitive dreams was realized.

Sometimes precognitive dreams predict events that take place only a few hours or days after the dream itself. At other times the event doesn't happen for years.

Many people have reported their precognitive dreams about the destruction of the World Trade Center. The Tribute in Light marked the anniversary of the attack.

Getting more from your dreams

Our dreams can be a rich source of information about what is happening in our lives. They reflect our anxieties and problems, and sometimes provide solutions. They can also give us messages and guidance, if we know how to interpret them. Learning from our dreams is an important part of our psychic development.

Recording your dreams will train your unconscious to remember them in detail.

REMEMBERING DREAMS

Although everyone dreams, not everyone remembers the experience. However, this is a situation that can easily be remedied with practice and patience. If your dreams are elusive, you can train yourself to remember them in detail. The best way to do this is to keep a dream journal and record your dreams in it every morning. At first, you may be

Capturing your dreams

If your dreams are hard to pin down, here are some tips on how to increase the likelihood of remembering them:

• Keep a notepad or your dream journal, plus a pen or pencil, next to your bed, so that they are easily accessible.

• Make sure you can easily reach a light switch, so that you can see what you're writing if you want to jot down a dream in the middle of the night.

• When you wake from a dream, don't move or speak. Stay in the same position in which you were sleeping. Mentally run through your dream and then write it down immediately. If you don't do this soon after waking, the dream may escape you.

• Sometimes a dream fades quickly after waking and is apparently gone forever. Yet it may return to you during the day, in which case you should write it down immediately before it vanishes again. Alternatively, you might remember it while you are falling asleep that night, in which case once again you should write it down. This will tell your unconscious to remember your dreams.

describing nothing more than a dim recollection of a particular emotion or physical sensation, but the very act of writing down your dreams will help you to remember them in increasing detail. Soon you will be able to recall each dream quite clearly, sometimes to the extent of remembering three or four dreams each night.

LUCID DREAMS

A lucid dream is an ordinary dream that differs in one respect: the sleeper is aware of being asleep and can consciously alter the course of the dream. This can be especially helpful for someone who has a repeated nightmare, because he is gradually able to train his brain to alter the outcome of the dream and therefore change its nightmarish quality. Lucid dreaming has the added benefit of enabling the dreamer to confront whatever is frightening him in his dream and, by doing so, to control and then lose his fears.

Lucid dreams have long been the subject of in-depth research. One of the pioneers of lucid dreaming was the Marquis d'Hervey de Saint-Denys in the 19th century. More recently, lucid dreams have been investigated at length by Stephen LaBerge and Lynne Levitan, among others, of the California-based Lucidity Institute. This was founded in 1987 by Dr. LaBerge and runs workshops on lucid dreaming.

Just as we can train ourselves to remember our ordinary dreams, so we can train ourselves to dream lucidly. The most important technique is to believe that you can experience lucid dreaming. If you unconsciously believe it is beyond your abilities, that is how it will remain. It helps to recognize what are often called "dreamsigns"—experiences in a dream that tell the dreamer she is asleep. These might be anything from realizing that she is in a strange body, to knowing that she's experiencing something that would be impossible in waking life.

Some people have reported experiencing more lucid dreams during brief naps than during a full night's sleep. These might be afternoon naps, but it seems that the most productive way to induce a lucid dream is to wake up 90 minutes earlier than usual in the morning, stay awake for 90 minutes and then to go back to sleep.

Lucid dreams are thought to be most likely to happen in the mornings.

Subtle energy

The body's subtle-energy system

At first glance, it seems that we humans consist entirely of our physical bodies. We have skin, bones, muscles, organs and many other tissues, all of which enable us to function and remain healthy. That is usually all we can see, so we believe that's all there is.

However, there is a lot more to each of us than that. In addition to our physical bodies, we have a subtle-energy system that is seven layers deep. It surrounds and penetrates our bodies and is called the aura (see also pages 82–83). This egg-shaped envelope of subtle energy is an extension of our physical bodies, although most of us can't see it and therefore aren't aware of it. It extends above our heads, below our feet, and beyond our backs and our fronts. We need it to remain healthy, just as we need our physical bodies.

The body's subtle-energy system is composed of an electromagnetic field and this is what enables us to make contact with the psychic plane. Although most of us aren't aware of

it, our subtle-energy systems are continually connecting with one another, transmitting and receiving complex messages.

THE AURA IN HISTORY

Although auras are often associated with New Age teachings, humankind has known about them for many centuries, both in the West and the East. Artists working in medieval Europe, such as Fra Angelico, Giusto de' Menabuoi and Giotto, painted religious scenes in which both humans and angels were surrounded by the most dazzling and beautiful auras. These auras were usually confined to the person's head, although in reality they completely surround the entire body.

Even in medieval Europe there was nothing new about people's knowledge of auras. Over 5,000 years ago mystical Indian teachings spoke of *prana*, which was considered to be the universal life force that flowed through all things. Equally, Chinese teachings from the

This painting by Fra Angelico clearly shows highly decorative halos.

same period talked of *ch'i*, which was the Chinese name for this energy that pervades everything and everyone. Many other cultures, and many different religions, believe in the existence of this universal energy.

KIRLIAN PHOTOGRAPHY

It is one thing to believe in auras and another to see them. During the 20th century various scientists developed mechanisms that enabled them to record and monitor the human aura. One of the most celebrated was Professor Semyon Kirlian, a Russian scientist whose pioneering work is still practiced today. Kirlian photography captures a person's aura on film, producing a fascinating image of the flares of light and energy that radiate from it.

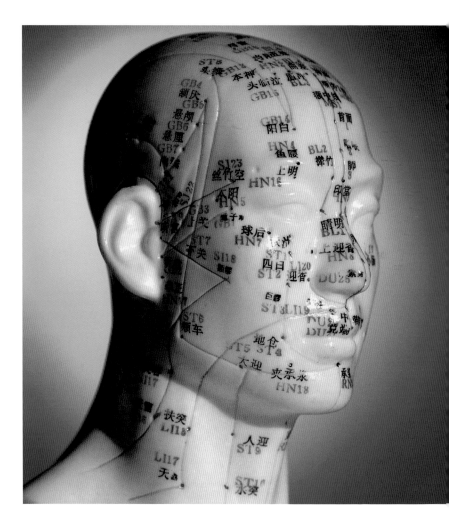

Meridians

In Chinese medicine, practitioners believe that *ch'i* (or the life force) flows through narrow channels in the body called *meridians*. These provide nourishment and support for the organs of the body. Meridians are important in acupuncture, in which very fine surgical needles are inserted into special acupuncture points on the body to relieve pain and cure health problems.

Although Chinese medicine has long embraced the concept of meridians in both humans and animals, Western medicine is still struggling with the idea. However, Western research eventually discovered that acupuncture points contain more nerves and blood vessels than their surrounding tissues.

Eager to discover whether meridians really do exist, scientists experimented by injecting radioactive tracers into the acupuncture points of humans and animals. The first scientist to do this, in the 1960s, was a Korean researcher called Dr. Kim Bong Han. He injected radioactive tracers into the acupuncture points of rabbits, revealing very tiny tubes that ran through the animals' organs and under their skin. These were identical to the meridians that were shown in ancient Chinese illustrations of rabbit meridians. Two decades later the same experiment was carried out by French researchers, this time using humans. As with the rabbits, the patterns and formations of the meridians in the human subjects exactly matched those shown in ancient Chinese acupuncture diagrams.

The chakras

The energy system of our bodies is much more complex than you might imagine. In addition to the seven layers within each person's aura, there are also seven chakras, or major energy centers, which run in a vertical line through the center of the body, from the bottom of the trunk up to the crown of the head. This can be a difficult concept to grasp at first, especially as the chakras do not manifest physically. However, they do exist at an energetic level, where they enable the body to regulate itself and operate efficiently. There are also twenty-one minor chakras, which are found mostly on the trunk, but also in the hands (these are particularly important when practicing healing techniques), head, knees and feet. And there are several higher chakras as well (see pages 80–81), with more to be discovered.

Chakra is the Sanskrit word for wheel, because the chakras are seen clairvoyantly as spinning wheels of energy. When a chakra spins perfectly,

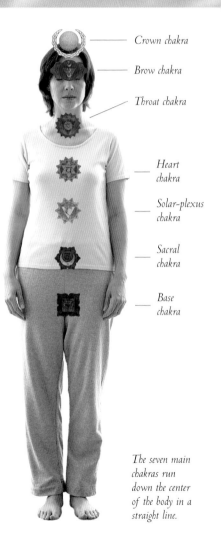

Crown chakra

Brow chakra

Throat chakra

Heart chakra

Solar-plexus chakra

Sacral chakra

Base chakra

The seven main chakras run down the center of the body in a straight line.

with no obstruction, distortion or sluggishness, it is functioning well and will not cause any physical, emotional or mental problems. However, these problems will start to manifest if the chakra stops spinning smoothly for some reason. You could think of it as a battery running down: everything controlled by that battery will also start to slow down.

WHAT ARE CHAKRAS?

The aura consists a network of fine lines, each of which is called a *nadi*. Chakras are the junctions where many of these lines of energy meet. The major chakras occur at the seven points where the greatest number of lines converge. Each major chakra is associated with specific parts of the body, with a time of physical development and with a color. Minor chakras occur at the twenty-one points where a smaller number of lines meet. These chakras have been found to coincide with areas in the body that are rich in nerve endings.

WHAT DO CHAKRAS DO?

Each chakra regulates a specific area of the body, as well as the emotions, mental outlook and spiritual purpose connected with that part of the body. For instance, if someone describes herself as "broken-hearted" over a love affair, it is her heart chakra that needs attention. Chakras also enable us to use our psychic gifts and to connect with one another on a psychic level. For instance, healers use their heart, hand and solar-plexus chakras when giving treatment.

The position of this woman's hands is giving energy to her sacral chakra.

The base chakra

Called the first chakra, this is located at the base of the trunk, in the perineum (the space between the genitals and the anus). As you might expect, this base or root chakra is very earthy and physical in nature. Indeed, it is the densest of the seven chakras and vibrates at the slowest rate because it has such a strong connection with the physical body.

FUNCTIONS OF THIS CHAKRA

One of the most important functions of the base chakra is to ground and stabilize. Without this essential connection with the earth, a person will be disconnected from her surroundings and emotionally adrift as well. She will probably have money problems, because she isn't part of the material world around her. (Equally, someone with a very dominant base chakra is usually profoundly materialistic, overtly sexual, very earthy and lacking in imagination and creativity.)

Another essential function of this chakra is to send energy up the line of

The base chakra or muladhara *rules our ability to be grounded in reality.*

chakras. Therefore if the base chakra isn't functioning properly or is undeveloped or blocked, the sacral chakra, which is its nearest neighbor, won't function well either because it won't receive enough energy.

The base chakra is connected to physical survival, and is strongly activated when someone is in danger. If

someone's base chakra does not function properly, she may be plagued by fears about her physical survival. She might also find it difficult to take care of herself, both emotionally and physically, especially if she failed to bond fully with her mother when she was a baby. Self-nurturing is connected with the base chakra.

The base chakra at a glance

Location in the body	The perineum
Areas of the body affected by this chakra	Bones, muscles, teeth, skin, base of spine, bone marrow, kidneys, rectum and bowel, legs and feet
Glandular system	Adrenals
Time of development	Between birth and five years old
Color	Red

The sacral chakra

Moving up the body from the base or first chakra, the second chakra is known as the sacral chakra. Its exact position is the width of two fingers below the navel. It doesn't vibrate as slowly as the base chakra, but nevertheless it is one of the three chakras associated with being physically in one's body (the other two are the base and solar-plexus chakras).

FUNCTIONS OF THIS CHAKRA

The sacral chakra is predominantly connected with our creativity in all its forms. It governs our ability to reproduce, so is intimately involved in conception and childbirth, and our ability to create with our imagination. Creativity comes in many different guises, and any form of creative expression, such as writing or painting, is governed by the sacral chakra in conjunction with the throat chakra (see pages 74–75).

Blockages in the sacral chakra manifest physically as reproductive problems, such as difficulties with

The sacral chakra or svadhisthara *governs all forms of creativity.*

menstruation or an inability to conceive. They can also show themselves in problems with sexuality, such as frigidity or an addiction to sex. Bladder and kidney ailments are also caused by a malfunctioning sacral chakra. Very often, such difficulties will be accompanied by a weakness in the throat chakra.

Another factor connected with this chakra is our attitude towards change and movement, whether physical or metaphorical. A blocked or weak chakra can lead to a rigid resistance to change, a desire to cling to the status quo at all costs. It can also cause a corresponding lack of flexibility in the body, such as a stiff back and hips.

The sacral chakra at a glance

Location in the body	Below the navel
Areas of the body affected by the chakra	Urinary and reproductive systems, lower back
Glandular system	Gonads
Time of development	Between three and eight years old
Color	Orange

The solar-plexus chakra

This is the third of the chakras, and the last one to be connected entirely with our physical selves. It vibrates at a higher rate than the two chakras beneath it. You will find it in your upper abdomen, beneath your sternum.

Many of us are aware of our solar-plexus chakra, even if we don't know what it's called, because it reacts so strongly to emotional stimuli. This is where we register and store our emotions—so we may experience butterflies in our stomachs when we're nervous, or may feel as though our stomachs turn a somersault when we are shocked.

FUNCTIONS OF THIS CHAKRA

This chakra is associated with our will, motivation and drive. This is where we are aware of our power (or lack of it) and where we feel free to be ourselves or feel that our individuality is blocked for some reason. The solar-plexus chakra

The solar-plexus chakra or manipura *is where we hold our emotions.*

dictates whether we are able to stand up to others who may try to dominate us, whether we cave in and let them walk all over us or whether we are the ones abusing our power. A poorly functioning solar-plexus chakra can make us feel inadequate and unable to cope with life's challenges. We might drift along, allowing others to make our decisions for us or rarely taking the initiative.

Since the solar-plexus chakra stores our emotions, it can harbor many difficult emotions that will eventually make us ill if we can't rid ourselves of them. Bitterness, resentment, rage that started in childhood, feelings of inadequacy and arrogance can all be stored here, eventually leading to physical problems in the areas of the body ruled by this chakra.

The solar-plexus chakra at a glance

Location in the body	Below the sternum
Areas of the body affected by the chakra	Stomach, liver, gallbladder
Glandular system	Pancreas
Time of development	Between 8 and 12 years old
Color	Yellow

The heart chakra

This is the middle chakra in our bodies and therefore provides the essential link between our human qualities (ruled by the base, sacral and solar-plexus chakras) and our divine qualities (ruled by the throat, brow and crown chakras). The heart chakra is located in the center of the chest, slightly to the right of the physical heart. It has two colors, pink and green, with green being the predominant color.

FUNCTIONS OF THIS CHAKRA

The heart chakra governs our ability to love others in the purest and most compassionate way we can. It is the chakra of unconditional love, and of love shown to the entire universe rather than directed at a particular person. We speak of people "coming from the heart," and when they do so they are functioning through their heart chakras.

When the heart chakra functions well, someone is warm, compassionate and empathic. There may be an attraction towards healing or some other

The heart chakra or anahata *is the point from which we send out unconditional love.*

form of service to humanity. Every chakra needs to open and close according to circumstance, but if the heart chakra is permanently open, it will lead to emotional exhaustion because the person is unable to shut off his emotions and is permanently "on call" for others. Conversely, if the heart chakra doesn't open properly, the person has difficulty in forgiving others and in giving unconditional love. He may be withholding his affection for others as a result of grief or bitterness. Blockages and other problems with the heart chakra can lead to breathing difficulties such as asthma and emphysema, poor circulation and cardiac irregularities.

The heart chakra at a glance

Location in the body	Center of chest
Areas of the body affected by the chakra	Heart, lungs, immune system, circulatory system, vagus nerve
Glandular system	Thymus
Time of development	Between 12 and 16 years old
Colors	Green and pink

The throat chakra

As you might imagine from its name, the throat chakra rules communication and self-expression in all its forms. This means it governs our ability, or lack of it, to say what we really think and to be truly honest, both with ourselves and with others. This chakra develops during our late teens, which is usually a time of self-discovery when we're learning to separate from our parents and develop our own ideas about life.

FUNCTIONS OF THIS CHAKRA

If we can't communicate with others, we feel as though there is something very important missing from our lives. There can be many emotional reasons for this inability to speak out, such as worrying that we will be criticized when we do say what we think, or that our ideas won't measure up to those of other people and that we will be ridiculed. We might also believe that our words carry such power that they will somehow

The throat chakra or vishuddha *governs our ability to communicate our thoughts.*

destroy other people if we really say what we think. We might have grown up in a family in which there was a tacit agreement not to be straightforward in case it offended someone, and where everyone resorted to euphemisms rather than plainly speaking the facts. The throat chakra is implicated in all these situations, and many others besides.

Alternatively, an over-developed throat chakra can lead to incessant chatter in which nothing of any importance is ever said. In this case, the person is trying to blot out silence with words, perhaps because he is frightened of what will happen if he allows himself to think.

Physical problems connected with a poorly functioning throat chakra can include sore throats, hoarseness and an under- or over-active thyroid.

The throat chakra at a glance

Location in the body	Neck
Area of the body affected by the chakra	Larynx
Glandular systems	Thyroid and parathyroid
Time of development	Between 16 and 21 years old
Color	Light or mid-blue

The brow chakra

The space between the eyes is the location of the third eye, which is another name for this chakra. The brow chakra is our inner eye, giving us inner vision so that we can tune into our intuition and connect with our personal spirit guides. It is the brow chakra that opens during creative and guided meditations, giving us glimpses of other worlds and different layers of existence. In common with the throat and crown chakras, the brow is one of the three chakras that links us to the Divine and to a spiritual life.

FUNCTIONS OF THIS CHAKRA

The brow chakra rules vision in all its forms, whether physical, intuitive, psychic or creative. Difficulties with the functioning of this chakra can lead to an inability to connect with our intuition, so that we feel disconnected from our inner guidance. We might discount our imaginative ideas as being foolish or not worth pursuing, or even blot them out as soon as they appear in

The brow chakra or ajna *regulates our intuition and inner wisdom.*

our minds because we are so convinced they're worthless. This means we also find it difficult to make contact with our guardian angels, and are therefore disconnected from an important source of guidance and love. There can be a physical impact too, such as poor eyesight, frequent eye strain, headaches or migraines.

Another difficulty caused by a weak brow chakra is that the person takes refuge in logic and rationality, to the extent that anything that doesn't fall into these categories is deemed foolish or nonsense. When this chakra is over-developed, someone may find it difficult to connect with so-called ordinary life, because metaphorically she has her head in the clouds.

The brow chakra at a glance

Location in the body	Between the eyes
Areas of the body affected by the chakra	Lower brain, vision, nervous system, ear, nose and throat
Glandular system	Pineal
Time of development	Usually between 21 and 26 years old
Colors	Deep indigo and purple

The crown chakra

Located on the top of the head, the crown chakra is highly sensitive. Even if you find it difficult to feel your other chakras, you are quite likely to sense this chakra. If anyone comes too close to it, you might feel a tingling in your scalp or a constriction in your head. This is the seventh chakra in the system, and it is the one that links us directly to the Divine, in whatever guise we may perceive this to be.

FUNCTIONS OF THIS CHAKRA

The crown chakra is our direct gateway to the higher realms, whether these comprise our soulmates who are in spirit (see pages 282–313), our spirit guides or God. When we practice healing or channeling, we consciously connect with the Divine through this chakra. The same thing happens unconsciously in prayer. However, when this Divine connection is weak or non-existent, we are plagued by thoughts

The crown chakra or sahasrara *enables us to link with the* Divine.

that God has deserted us or that there is no such thing as God.

The crown chakra affects the health of the brain, and when it is impaired or closed down, a person can experience bouts of depression and despair. There might also be neurological disorders of the brain, such as epilepsy or some mental illness.

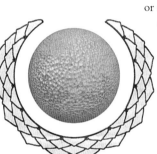

Just as the base chakra (see pages 66–67) is connected with the mother, so the crown chakra is connected with the father. A difficult relationship with the father, who might be absent or over-controlling, can cause this chakra to close down. There can be problems in accepting or abiding by other people's authority, if the crown chakra is not functioning well.

The crown chakra at a glance

Location in the body	Top of the head
Area of the body affected by the chakra	Upper brain
Glandular system	Pituitary
Time of development	After the age of 26 years
Colors	Violet and white

The higher chakras

In addition to the seven chakras that are located in the human body itself, there are now considered to be several other chakras as well, although the exact number is still open to discussion. This is because they are still being discovered, and in some cases there is still a certain amount of confusion about their location in the human aura. However, in no way does this reduce the power of these chakras, nor the integrity of the people who work with them. They are known as the "higher chakras," because they relate to our higher purpose and higher selves. Sometimes they are referred to as the "New Age" chakras, to distinguish them from the traditional seven-chakra system.

Occasionally, you will find that the heart, throat, brow and crown chakras are referred to as "higher chakras" due to their physical location in the aura. Here, however, the term refers to the new chakras described on these pages.

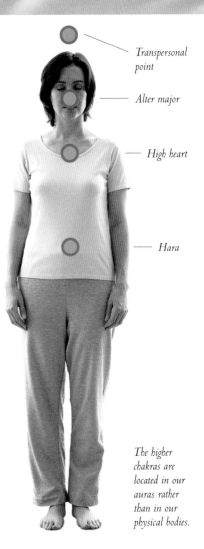

Transpersonal point

Alter major

High heart

Hara

The higher chakras are located in our auras rather than in our physical bodies.

THE TRANSPERSONAL POINT

This chakra is located above our heads, so it is part of our aura (see pages 82–83) and has no apparent connection with our physical bodies at all. It is thought to be the link between our egos (or conscious minds) and our higher selves, and when we connect with it we are able to view our lives from a more dispassionate and objective perspective.

For instance, it is this point that enables us to gain some idea of the soul lessons that we can learn from the difficult situations in which we sometimes find ourselves. Activating this chakra through meditation gives us a better overview of our lives and the purpose of our current incarnation.

THE HARA

Although the location of this chakra, near the navel, suggests that it penetrates the physical body in the same way as the seven major chakras, in fact it exists only in the aura. It is a vortex of energy located in the aura between the sacral and solar-plexus chakras. Although we all have a hara, it is not necessarily active.

Healers who work with their hara experience a powerful healing energy that they often find is stronger than when they work with their heart chakras.

THE ALTER MAJOR

This chakra is located at the back of the head, near the nape of the neck, and is connected to the old brain cortex. You will find the alter major around the nose on the front of the face. It helps us to connect with our instincts and intuition, so is an important chakra to activate if you wish to practice psychic work.

THE HIGH HEART CHAKRA

Located in the aura between the heart and throat chakras, this higher chakra is also known as the "soul seat" and the "thymic" chakra. The high heart chakra helps us to activate our higher consciousness, and it also regulates our intentions. These move from the heart chakra, through the high heart chakra, to the throat chakra where they are turned into action. The high heart chakra can become blocked by bottled up emotions.

The aura

The aura is the envelope of subtle energy that surrounds each living and inanimate object on the planet. As humans, we literally can't exist without our auras, because they are an energetic extension of our bodies. Auras are energy fields, holding a tremendous amount of information about us. They consist of very fine electromagnetic energy, which is easily visible to clairvoyants. However, we can all train ourselves to see our auras, as you will discover later in this section (see pages 84–85).

THE LAYERS OF THE AURA

When you first learn to see your aura you will probably only discern a small blue layer of energy next to your body. However, there is a lot more to your aura than that. There is some debate about the number of layers within a human aura, but it's generally agreed there are seven. Each layer is finer in energy, and vibrates at a higher frequency, than the previous one.

Therefore the densest layer of the aura, called the etheric body, is closest to the body, while the finest layer, called the ketheric template, is farthest away from the body. Although the layers might appear to be separate from one another, each one overlaps the layer or layers beneath it.

TUNING INTO YOUR AURA

Your aura has an electromagnetic field and you can train yourself to become sensitive to this field and therefore to become aware when someone or something penetrates it. This is essential in psychic work, when you are continually tuning into your aura to gain impressions and sensations about what is happening around you.

Although you might imagine that your physical body influences your aura, in fact the reverse is true. Clairvoyants who have observed human fetuses developing in their mothers' wombs have described how the layers of the aura are formed first, thereby creating a template for the physical cells to copy. Equally, any ailments or illnesses that we develop first appear in our auras as blocks of mental or emotional energy. If we are unable to shift these, whether consciously or unconsciously, they eventually begin to affect our physical bodies.

Etheric body ——————
Emotional body ——————
Mental body ——————
Astral layer ——————
Etheric template ——————
Celestial body ——————
Ketheric template ——————

Our auras are composed of seven layers. The densest layer is the etheric body, which lies next to our physical bodies.

How to see and sense the aura

You may not yet be able to sense or see your aura, but it is easy to learn how to do this. People with the gift of clairvoyance may be able to see auras naturally, with no effort, but the rest of us have to train ourselves to detect them. This is a much easier process than you might imagine.

LEARN TO SEE YOUR AURA

Start by looking at the aura around your hands, and then you can use the same process to view your aura around other parts of your body. At first you will only see your etheric body, which is the aura nearest your physical body, but with practice you will see more layers of your aura.

1 Sit in a comfortable chair, facing a pale, plain wall. Don't sit in direct sunlight or with an artificial light shining on you. Ground and balance yourself (see pages 24–25).

2 Stretch out your right arm, with the back of your hand facing you. Now look at the space between your splayed fingers and the wall, without looking directly at either of them. Allow your eyes to relax.

3 You will start to see a fuzzy white or gray outline around your fingers. This is your aura. Continue to look at the space between your fingers and the wall. The gray or white outline will start to change color, and will usually turn blue.

VIEW THE AURA AROUND YOUR HEAD

Once you can see the aura around your hands, turn your attention to viewing the aura around your head.

1 Stand in front of a mirror, with a plain pale wall behind you. Ground and balance yourself, as before.

2 Look at the space above your head, letting your eyes relax. You will soon start to see a fuzzy grey or white outline around your head, which will then change into a shade of blue. This is your etheric body.

SENSE YOUR AURA

Another way to work with your aura is to sense it with your hands. This is good fun and the quick results are encouraging. You can use this exercise as a way of preparing yourself to carry out healing (see pages 124–155).

1 Set aside some time when you won't be disturbed, then ground and balance yourself, as before.

2 Hold the palms of your hands close together, without letting them touch. Now move your palms apart and then bring them together again, always taking note of how the energy between your hands feels. Continue to move them backwards and forwards, taking them slightly farther apart each time.

3 As you work, you will notice a sensation building up in the palms of your hands. For instance, they may tingle or feel hot. You will also feel the energy building up in the space between your hands; it will feel elastic and bouncy, and as you move your hands close together, you will sense a slight resistance between them. This is your aura!

SENSE YOUR CHAKRAS

When you have learned to sense your aura, you can progress to sensing your chakras. It is exactly the same process, but the feeling you get will be different.

1 Set aside some time when you can be alone, then ground and balance yourself, as before.

2 Choose a particular chakra to work on, such as your solar-plexus chakra (see pages 70–71) or your heart chakra (see pages 72–73).

3 Hold your hand about 12 in. (30 cm) away from the relevant area of your body, then start to move it gently backwards and forwards. You are sensing the edge of your aura. Gently move your hand towards your body until it meets some resistance. This means that you're making contact with that chakra's energy.

4 Continue to sense the chakra's energy, and notice how different it feels from the surrounding aura. For instance, the aura around the chakra may feel quite dense and solid, compared to a much lighter sensation away from the chakra. You may also feel a pressure in your body as you press on the chakra's energy.

Aura shapes and colors

Your aura is not an amorphous blob. In its ideal state, it is a perfect egg shape, well-balanced, with no lopsided areas and no signs of damage. It stretches a couple of inches above your head and extends beneath your feet, encasing you completely in its protective shield.

However, not everyone's aura is always perfect. An aura can get out of alignment, with one side much thinner than the other, or it can appear to shrink so that it no longer stretches down beneath a person's feet, but instead might stop at knee-level. It varies in color too, according to the person's mood and state of health, although it always has one predominant color. There is no ideal color for an aura, because each one reflects a different personality type and way of looking at the world.

TUNING INTO DIFFERENT COLORS

As you become more sensitive, you will notice that you become increasingly attuned to the colors in your environment. There will be days when you feel drawn to some colors and repelled by others. You might also feel a craving for a specific color, in which case you can consult the chart to understand why you need that color and learn more about the chakra to which it refers. For instance, a sudden attraction to red might signify a need to be more grounded and to have more energy. You might like to satisfy that craving by wearing clothes or jewelry in the relevant color, or by placing a vase of suitably colored flowers on your desk or by your bed. You may also feel compelled to eat foods of a particular color, such as bananas, yellow peppers and pears. Follow your instincts in this.

Consider the colors in your home as well. Do you like them? The more you pay attention to the colors in your life, the more you will learn about yourself and about the ever-changing state of your chakras.

The shapes of the aura

When you learn to view or sense an aura, you will soon notice that not every aura has a perfect egg shape. Here are some of the different aura shapes that you can expect to find, as well as suggestions concerning what they might mean and the treatment that they may require (see pages 94–95 for ways to heal the aura).

Shape	Meaning	Treatment
Lopsided aura	Wariness; fear; lack of trust	Plump up the narrow part and push in the fatter part
Flattened area over crown chakra	Depression	Gently tease out the dented part of the aura
Aura stops at knees	Lack of grounding; fear; lack of connection with surroundings and base chakra	Pull the aura down to below the feet; perform the grounding exercise (see pages 24–25)
Jagged edge to aura	Lack of boundaries; physical damage to body	Smooth over the jagged edges

The colors of the aura

Each of us has a predominant color in our aura, although other colors may come and go according to our state of health and our emotions. Here are some of the predominant colors you can expect to see in someone's aura, with brief descriptions of what these colors say about the person and the chakras to which they are connected. Use your intuition to expand on these descriptions.

	Color	Meaning	Chakra
	Red	Energy, action, leadership, innovation	Base
	Orange	Optimism, confidence, emotional warmth	Sacral
	Yellow	Communication, creativity, mental agility, gregariousness	Solar-plexus

	Color	Meaning	Chakra
	Green	Love, kindness, peacefulness, a love of nature, a need for harmony	Heart
	Pink	Affection, compassion, strong spirituality	Heart
	Blue	Consideration, idealism, ethical values, spiritual knowledge	Throat
	Indigo/purple	Love, psychic ability, intuition, spiritual purpose	Brow
	White	Spiritual evolution, connection with the Divine, humanitarianism	Crown

Cleansing and healing the aura

Once you become aware of your aura and are able to sense it, you will want to take care of it. You will wish to clean it on a regular basis, especially after having a difficult experience. And you will want to heal it if you notice any problems with it, such as hot or cold spots, or tears in it. These procedures need only take a short amount of time each day, but you will soon notice the difference in your energy levels. You may also find that you're able to ward off ailments before they become established in your body, because you will have cleared the corresponding energetic blocks in your aura.

CLEANSING YOUR AURA

The best way to ensure that problems don't build up in your aura is to clean it every day. This is especially important if you work with other people, or travel each day on public transport, because then you will pick up a lot of energy. Regular maintenance of your aura will help to prevent any serious problems accumulating in it.

DAILY CLEANSING

You can carry out this exercise whenever you feel the need for it, or set aside a special time each day for it.

1 Sit comfortably, with both feet flat on the floor. Ground and balance yourself (see pages 24–25).

2 Imagine a large disc of energy, which is much wider than your body, hovering high above your head. If it helps, you could imagine that you can hear it humming.

3 Now imagine the disc slowly moving downwards, so that it begins to pass through your aura and your physical body. As it progresses downwards, it is collecting all the

negative emotions, thoughts and experiences that have become trapped in your aura.

4 Picture the disc reaching your feet and then passing through the floor beneath you, taking all the energetic debris with it. Know that the earth will absorb the discarded energy and transform it into positive energy.

5 Repeat the exercise if you feel it's necessary. When you have finished, sit quietly for a few moments before stretching your arms and legs and coming fully back into your body.

HEALING YOUR AURA

If you detect any tears or other problems with your aura, you can heal them. We have already discussed some of the problems you might find in your aura and ways to heal them (see pages 88–89). Here is another exercise that you can perform when you sense there might be something wrong with your aura, but aren't sure what it is.

1 Sit comfortably in a chair, with both feet on the ground. Choose a time when you won't be disturbed, so that you can relax. Ground and balance yourself, as before.

2 Close your eyes and tune into your aura, gaining a good sense of it being around you. Imagine it extending away from your body in all directions, and above your head and beneath your feet.

3 Now ask for healing energy to be sent to any area of your aura that needs help. Trust your intuition and know that the healing is being directed to the relevant section of your aura. Imagine that a ball of sparkling, golden light is moving over the damaged part of your aura, gently healing it. If there are tears in your aura, imagine them being mended by the golden light.

4 Let the golden light move from one section of your aura to the next, healing each one in turn. Do your best to be aware of this process as it happens, because that will sharpen your intuition and psychic abilities. When the golden light stops moving or disappears, the healing is complete.

5 Give thanks for the healing and ground yourself again. Slowly open your eyes, then stretch your arms and legs so that you return to your body.

Psychic protection

What is psychic protection?

We are all sensitive to atmospheres, even if to differing degrees. We can have lovely experiences in which we happily soak up the atmosphere around us, and stressful ones in which we feel uncomfortably immersed in something we don't like. Sometimes we're able to rid ourselves of the energetic residue without much trouble, but there are occasions when it is much more difficult to shift this. If you have ever watched a film that left you with an unpleasant feeling that you couldn't shake off, or have endlessly rehashed a difficult conversation in your mind long after the real dialogue ended, you will know what this feels like. In cases like these, you need to give yourself some

A Buddhist mala can be used to give psychic protection.

psychic protection. It acts in exactly the same way as a raincoat protects us from the rain, or a pair of sunglasses deflects the harsh rays of the sun.

Rose quartz is a particularly good choice if you're looking for a protective crystal.

DIFFERENT FORMS OF PROTECTION

It is important to find a form of psychic protection that suits you, and which you can summon up in an instant whenever you need it. One form of protection—which appeals to many millions of people of differing faiths around the world—is to say a prayer. You don't have to belong to an organized religion in order to do this: many people who would never describe themselves as religious find that they start to pray when they need help. You can say a prayer aloud or in your head, depending on the circumstances. It can be a formal prayer that you already know, or one that you make up on the spot. Keep saying it until you feel better.

Another option is to wear something that gives you protection. This could be a religious symbol, or it might be a crystal, such as a rose quartz or a black tourmaline. You will find many other techniques described in this section, at least one of which will be perfect for you.

Why do I need psychic protection?

Imagine that your aura is a psychic magnet. It attracts emotions and thoughts, some of which are beneficial, while others are less harmonious. We are happy to absorb the delightful experiences into our auras, but have problems processing the difficult experiences. These can manifest in many ways, including bad dreams, repetitive thoughts, unsettled emotions or uncharacteristic behavior. Sometimes we can feel as though something is stuck to us, or we become drained after being with someone who is emotionally very needy or controlling.

OTHER PEOPLE'S ENERGY

If you spend a lot of time with other people, perhaps because your job brings you into daily contact with the general public or you are working in one of the service professions, you need to give

You should never do any psychic work without protecting yourself first.

yourself regular psychic protection. This will enable you to repel any negative energy that is around you, while absorbing the pleasant energy. However, psychic protection is helpful no matter what you do each day, and with practice it will become a regular part of your daily routine.

Psychic work

It is important to protect yourself whenever you want to develop or use your psychic abilities. Mediums (also known as sensitives), who are able to contact the spirit world with such ease, always have spirit guides who act as gatekeepers, filtering out unwelcome and meddlesome spirits. When you first start to work on your psychic abilities, you will need to be your own gatekeeper because you won't have learned to tune into your own spirit guides. And, for all you know, a mischievous spirit may be pretending to be your spirit guide, just as there are people on Earth who pretend to be something they are not. The fact that someone is in spirit is not an automatic guarantee that they have loving and helpful intentions. Some spirits are lovely, while others are very unpleasant. You must learn how to tell the difference. One way to do this is to ask the spirit if he comes from God. Ask him three times. Spiritual law decrees that he will tell the truth in his third answer.

Breathing

Before you begin to learn how to give yourself some psychic protection, you must learn how to control your breathing. Then, if you find yourself in a difficult situation or one that frightens you, you will be able to use your breathing to keep calm and become centered. This will greatly aid all your psychic protection techniques, because they won't be very effective if you are breathing rapidly due to anxiety or tension.

Most of us take shallow breaths from the top third of our lungs. As a result, our blood is not as well oxygenated as it could be, and we don't expel the waste products from our lungs in the way that nature intended. Therefore the following breathing exercise has physical, as well as psychic, benefits.

MEASURED BREATHING

This is a very simple exercise, which you can practice at any time, so that it becomes a habit. You could even practice it while watching television. It is especially useful to do this exercise whenever you catch yourself breathing in a shallow way, even if you aren't feeling tense at the time.

1 Become conscious of your breathing, taking note of whether it's very shallow or whether you are holding your breath.

2 Take a deep breath, then slowly expel all the air in your lungs. Let the air flow back into your lungs without forcing it.

3 Pause for a couple of beats, then slowly breathe out. Devote the same amount of time to the in-breath as the out-breath, such as five beats. Establish a gentle rhythm, so that you are breathing in for five beats, pausing for two beats, then exhaling for five beats, and pausing again for two beats before beginning the cycle once more.

4 As you breathe in this measured way, feel the tension draining out of your body and your heart beating more slowly. Enjoy the calm, tranquil sensation that this gives you.

Psychic protection exercises

There are many ways to protect yourself psychically. Your best option is to practice each of the exercises on the following pages to find the ones you prefer. You can adapt them if you wish, but always remember that you should do so while maintaining a calm, loving attitude. If you protect yourself with an

THE PSYCHIC BUBBLE

This is a very popular technique because it's simple and it works. Try to get into the habit of practicing it on a regular basis (preferably every day), so that your psychic bubble becomes increasingly strong. It will then offer you greater protection whenever you really need it. Ideally you should have your psychic bubble in place before you start each day, rather than having to surround yourself with it in a hurry when you realize you need it.

1 Breathe slowly and regularly, then ground and balance yourself (see pages 24–25).

2 Imagine that you are surrounded by a bubble of psychic energy, which protects you from any negative influences, while allowing positive emotions to flow between you and other people.

3 Make sure the bubble stretches above your head and below your feet, and that it meets behind your back. Picture it as

aggressive technique, you may attract even more aggression in others as a result. Remember, like attracts like.

PROTECTING YOUR BELONGINGS

There are simple ways to protect your belongings from other people or from harmful influences. For instance, you could imagine that the item is completely surrounded by a large psychic bubble (see below). You can do this for anything you own, such as your house or your car. Throughout the day keep checking mentally that the bubble is still in place and is intact.

being elastic, so that it can retract towards you when necessary, or extend outwards whenever you're feeling safe and comfortable.

4 Visualize the color of your psychic bubble. In ordinary situations, you may like to picture it being made of white or golden light. In more stressful situations, when you need increased protection, imagine that the bubble is made up of seven layers, each one a different color of the rainbow.

Ask for angelic assistance if you're worried about the security of your home.

Another option is to appoint psychic guardians to keep watch over your possessions. You can vary your choice of guardians according to the circumstances. For instance, you could choose fairies to take care of the plants in your garden if you're worried about them being damaged or stolen, or ask for animal guardians to watch over your pets whenever you're away from home. Alternatively, you could cultivate a network of angels, who can help you in many ways. Although you might think such celestial beings aren't tough enough to protect your house from burglars, in fact they are well equipped to cope with all eventualities. However, if you would prefer to choose what you consider to be more intimidating guardians when you feel they're necessary, you could appoint some big, burly guardians to protect your car when you leave it in unfamiliar car parks. And each night, before you go to sleep, you could ask angels to watch over your home and family. Whenever you leave your home, you could ask for it to be surrounded on all sides by gatekeepers who will repel unwanted visitors.

APPOINTING PSYCHIC GUARDIANS

1 Breathe slowly and calmly to become centered, then ground and balance yourself, as before.

2 Ask to be sent some psychic guardians, who will protect whatever you are concerned about. Visualize them arriving and taking up their positions. Know that they are there. Thank them for coming to your aid.

3 When you no longer need them, thank them again for their help and tell them they are free to leave.

The psychic mirror

There may be times when you feel that you need additional help in protecting yourself from the energies of the people around you. One very effective way to do this is to mentally put up a mirror between you and the person concerned. This will reflect the person's behavior back to him, thereby deflecting it away from you.

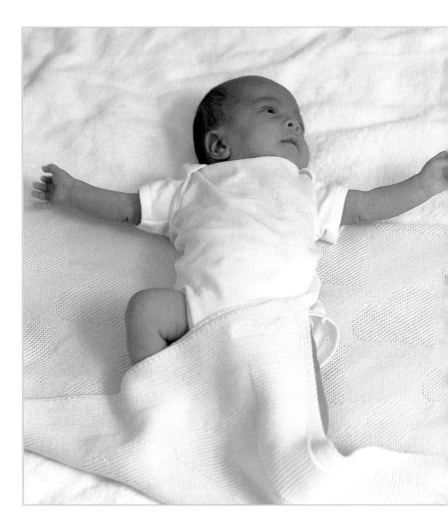

PROTECTION THROUGH LOVE

The psychic mirror protection (see page 107) is very effective, but it can also feel slightly aggressive. If you're worried about making a difficult situation worse than ever, or you instinctively feel that sending someone love is a better option than sending his own energy straight back to him, you can try the following exercise. It is a reminder that love is the strongest force in the universe.

1 Find a time when you won't be disturbed. Ground and balance yourself, as before. Then breathe slowly and regularly.

2 In your mind's eye, picture the person you are having problems with. Send this person your love.

3 If any angry thoughts come into your mind, or memories of problems you are experiencing with this person, gently send these thoughts on their way. Focus again on the person and send him your love. If this is difficult, it should help to imagine him as a small, vulnerable child. Alternatively, you can think of someone or something you truly love, such as your partner or your pet, and then direct the loving feelings that you experience towards the person who is causing you problems. The more you practice this exercise, the easier it will become. It will also start to transform your relationship with the person concerned.

A psychic warning system

The more practiced you are in the art of tuning into your emotions and thoughts, and in realizing that something unpleasant has touched your aura, the more efficient your psychic warning system will become. The key is to be grounded and balanced whenever possible. You will then know when you are thrown off-balance by outside forces, because you will suddenly feel different.

Making a habit of being centered and grounded is important for another reason, too. Some people believe that they are under psychic attack from another person when in fact they are generating the unpleasant emotions themselves. For instance, they may get angry about someone, while denying this to themselves, and then attribute their churned-up feelings to psychic attack from the person in question.

WARNING SENSATIONS

If you make a habit of being calm and balanced, you will quickly know when you need to protect yourself against

something or someone. Pay attention to the signals that your body sends you, such as sudden tension in your stomach, tingling on your skin or an apparently inexplicable agitation. If you are aware of your spirit guides and regularly work with them, they will also send you a warning when you are in the presence of an unpleasant or negative energy.

Sometimes you will experience strange sensations that you can't explain at the time, but which later turn out to be your aura defending itself. For instance, when walking through a wood in which something unpleasant is taking place, you might become aware of a protective sheath covering your crown chakra. This might feel like a flannel or a hat, and no matter how often you brush it away, it will return until you're out of the wood. When this happens, you can be sure that you are being given psychic protection.

Sometimes your body's physical sensations will tell you to protect yourself psychically.

Clearing negative energy

There will inevitably be times when you forget to put your psychic bubble (see pages 104–105), or other form of psychic protection, in place and as a result accumulate some negative energy. This might happen when you have a difficult conversation with someone, when you watch a disturbing news bulletin or when you take a seat on the bus and discover that you have picked up the previous occupant's unsettling energy. Don't worry, because it's easy to

rid yourself of all this energy. You simply need to know how to do it.

WASHING IT AWAY

One of the best and simplest ways to clear yourself of negative energy is to have a bath or shower. As you wash yourself, imagine that you are washing away the negative energy that you have

Having a bath is one of the most effective ways to cleanse your aura.

Washing clothes and drying them in the fresh air removes any negative energy that may be trapped in them.

attracted. Make sure you wash your hair at the same time. As you watch the water disappearing down the drain, know that it is carrying the negative energy with it.

For additional help, you can add some sea salt to your bath. Salt is very cleansing and is especially helpful when it feels as though someone's energy has become stuck to you and you can't shake it off. You can also add a few drops of walnut Bach Flower Remedy or fringed violet Australian Bush Flower Essence (see pages 172–175) to your bath water to clean your aura.

CLEAN CLOTHES

Our clothes hold on to our energetic residues, so it's a good idea to keep them fresh and aired. If you have had a difficult day, perhaps because you had an argument with someone, ideally you should wash all your clothes before wearing them again. If that isn't possible, at least take them outside and give them a thorough shake to knock out the negative energy, then leave them to air on hangers. If you can leave them in the open air, in the sunshine, so much the better. Remember to give your shoes a good airing, too.

You can do the same thing with your bedding after you have had a nightmare or a restless night's sleep. Give all the bedclothes (including your pillows) a good shake, then leave them in a sunny place for at least one hour.

KEEPING ACTIVE

If energy is stuck, it starts to stagnate. This can happen quite quickly, so it's a good idea to be active each day. Exercise keeps your energy moving and helps to prevent a build-up of anything negative. Even a short walk around the room— or, better still, around the block—will make you feel clearer and fresher.

AFTER AN ARGUMENT

Arguments inevitably stir up lots of negative energy, even if they end amicably. You need to clear this energy —not only from the room or area in which the argument took place, but from your own aura. To clear the room, open the windows to let in some fresh air and then clear the atmosphere in

The penetrating sound created by a singing bowl is an excellent purifier of energy.

whichever way feels most appropriate. You could do this by walking around the room and clapping your hands to break up the energy. Or you could play a favorite piece of sacred music to purify the atmosphere. Another option is to put a few drops of Rescue Remedy in a spray bottle filled with water, and spray this into the room.

You can also use a singing bowl, if you have one: this beaten metal bowl is struck with a wooden beater to create a resonant note and has healing and cleansing qualities. Stand in each corner of the room in turn and strike the singing bowl. The resonating sound will help to disperse the negative energy. Then repeat the exercise in the middle of the room.

After clearing the room's energy, you can add a final touch by placing a small bowl of sea salt in the center of the room and leaving it there for as long as possible. The salt will absorb the negative energies, so be sure to dispose of it carefully—don't put it back in the salt grinder! Instead, bury it outside.

A bowl of sea salt will help to cleanse the atmosphere of a room after an argument.

Blessings and affirmations

One wonderful way to introduce more psychic protection into your life, and to attract positive experiences, is to bless everything and everyone you encounter. This can feel strange and unfamiliar at first, and possibly even patronizing. But, as you get used to making a simple blessing over your food at each meal, or blessing every difficult situation that you meet, you will soon start to feel more comfortable with the process. You will also realize that it has a deep-seated emotional impact on you and brings you many benefits.

BLESSING YOUR FOOD AND DRINK

It is natural in religious and spiritual societies to bless food before you eat it. For instance, Christians say a grace over their food, to thank God for having

Try to get into the habit of blessing everything that you eat and drink.

provided it. Buddhists always bow before and after eating, to give thanks for their food. In Ayurveda—a healing system that originated in India more than 5,000 years ago and aims to balance the subtle energies of the body, with special importance placed on diet —the food is not only blessed, but cleared of all karmic debt before it is eaten. Even if you don't have a religious faith, you will still receive benefits from blessing all the food you eat, whether it's a three-course meal or a chocolate biscuit with your afternoon cup of tea.

All you need to do is to perform a simple blessing ritual at the start of each meal. Choose whatever feels natural to you and know that this blessing has worked. For instance, you could make the sign of an equal-sided cross over the food with your hand, or you could raise your plate to your forehead. Ideally you should also speak the blessing out loud, which increases its strength and impact.

Liquids also respond well to blessings, which is why there are so many sacred wells throughout the world. Water can easily be magnetized by blessing it (thereby holding its energy and retaining the blessing), but there is no reason why you should stop at blessing water. Bless your fruit juice, tea, coffee, milk . . . even your glass of wine.

Affirmations

An affirmation is a positive saying that you repeat to yourself over and over again in order to transmit its message to your subconscious. Energy follows thought, so a repeated affirmation will always manifest as energy. Once you start to practice this, you will begin to understand the importance of monitoring what you think. If you often focus on illness or poverty, that is what you will manifest sooner or later; if you focus on health, abundance, happiness or anything else that you want, that is what you will attract. Here are some tips on making affirmations:

• Choose the present tense. You don't want to tell your subconscious that you will be more joyful at some point in the future: you want to tell it you're joyful right this minute. Try something like "I attract joy into my life now."

• Delete any negative words from your affirmations—you want your affirmation to be positive. For example, if you want to recover from a nasty bout of flu, don't say, "I am recovering from flu," for your subconscious will focus on the word "flu," and not on the word "recovering." Use an affirmation such as "I have perfect health now."

• Don't ask for something that will cause harm, whether to another person or yourself. If you're affirming that your friendships will improve, you don't want something awful to happen to your current friends. Therefore you need to choose your words carefully and add a rider, such as "for the highest good of all concerned."

• Say your affirmation out loud, for at least five minutes every day. Say it lovingly and feel its truth within your heart. Know that it will come true and anticipate the joy you'll feel when it does. Don't confuse your subconscious by giving it mixed messages, such as adding, "I wonder if it will really happen."

Overcoming fear

Some of us are more fearful than others. Some of us go through life permanently poised to cope with the disasters and problems that we believe are lurking round every corner. We can fret about anything—whether it's the fear that heavy rain will spoil our planned picnic; that our partner will run off with someone who is so much more attractive than we are; or that our proposed house move will fall through at the last minute.

Living in a personal world that is governed by fear has a bad effect on our health. It undermines our immune systems, making us more susceptible to illness. It interferes with our metabolism, flooding our bloodstreams with too much of the fight-or-flight hormones, cortisol and adrenalin. It interrupts our sleep patterns, plays havoc with our digestive systems and has many other effects on us, too. Some of us may feel that we're under psychic attack when really we're overreacting and imagining the worst.

What is perhaps most frightening about fear is that it attracts fearful circumstances. Like attracts like, so you are more likely to experience unpleasant situations if you are already fearful. In effect, you are programming yourself to experience situations that will justify the fear you feel. So how can you break out of this vicious cycle?

A MULTI-FACETED APPROACH

There are many ways to face your fears and increase your confidence. The first is to look closely at what you're frightened of, and why. Do you fear that you will lose everything you have because, deep down, you feel you don't deserve it? Do you think you will be punished for your misdeeds or bad behavior? If your fears are very deep-seated or stem from a past trauma, you may need professional help in dealing with them. If there is a constructive solution to your fear, act on it. Taking flower remedies that are designed to deal with fear will also help you.

*Fear can become a prison if you allow it to gain
control of you.*

Building confidence

Once you have started to realize how anxious you are, you can replace your anxiety with more positive emotions. Here are some suggestions:

Restrictive measures
• Stop reading the newspaper or watching the news for a week and notice how much better you feel as a result. Avoid television programs, films, magazines and books that dwell on misery or violence.

• Keep away from people who are very negative and who like to focus on the horrible things in life. Spend time with people who make you laugh and feel good. If you don't know any, you need to find some new friends!
• Limit your worrying time to five minutes each day. Whenever you worry outside this time, dismiss the concern from your mind. You will soon realize that you have forgotten to do any worrying at all.

Pro-active measures

• Pay attention to your thoughts. Every time you catch yourself thinking something negative or fearful, replace that thought with something positive.
· Discover a fresh hobby or interest, so that you have something new and fun to think about. Enjoy the time you spend on it and don't feel guilty.
• Take more exercise, even if you only go for a brisk walk each day. Exercising releases endorphins, the feel-good hormones, into your bloodstream. You will notice a difference in your health and weight as well.
• Develop a spiritual practice. This could be anything from attending your local church (but only if you enjoy going there) to reading

Be choosy about the company you keep and avoid people who are negative or gloomy.

Do your best to build some regular exercise into your daily routine.

personal-development books.
• Learn to meditate (see pages 44–45). Meditation has untold health benefits and brings a deep sense of peace and relaxation. It also means you have to set aside some time for yourself each day.
• Take up yoga. Not only will this increase your body's suppleness and strength, but it will also improve your breathing and can give you a more spiritual outlook on life.

Energy healing

What is energy healing?

Energy healing has been practiced for millennia. There is nothing new about it, despite the current proliferation of healing techniques and healing schools. Put very simply, energy healing is the practice of changing someone's physical, emotional, mental or spiritual state by altering the energy around him. Healing always brings change of some sort, although it may be on a level that the patient is not expecting.

We are all healers, although most of us don't realize it. If you have ever comforted a tearful child who has hurt herself, you will have given her healing. Maybe you gave her a hug, rubbed her bumped elbow or told her that you would kiss it better. Those are all forms of healing. We often talk of doctors having a "good bedside manner," which means that they comfort and reassure their patients. Even before the doctor writes out a prescription, the patient may start to feel better. There are many possible psychological reasons for this, but there is also the distinct possibility

that the doctor is a natural healer, which is why he was initially drawn to the medical profession. Unfortunately this doesn't mean that everyone working in medicine is motivated primarily by the desire to heal: some people are looking for other gratification, such as power, status or financial gain.

DOES HEALING ALWAYS WORK?

Healing always creates some form of change, so it always works at some level. Some people experience miraculous cures when given healing. These cures are often so dramatic that they appear to defy the laws of allopathic (conventional) medicine, usually resulting in bewildered doctors believing that they were mistaken in their original diagnoses. Other people experience definite relief from their symptoms, but don't have a complete cure. Some find little physical benefit from the healing, but discover that other areas of their lives start to improve or that long-

When giving healing, you can place your hands on or off a person's body.

standing problems are suddenly resolved. There are no guarantees about how healing will affect a patient, just as there are no guarantees about how he will respond to conventional medicine.

Types of healing

Healing takes many forms. There is simple psychic or energy healing, which involves the healer channeling energy from a higher source and transferring it to the aura of the patient. There is the power of prayer, in which someone prays that healing will take place. A similar technique is to invoke a religious figure, such as saying, "Jesus Christ manifests perfect order in me now." Affirmations (see pages 116–119), or positive statements, such as "I have perfect health now," can also bring about healing. There are other healing techniques as well, such as healing with crystals or flower remedies. In fact, all complementary therapies, as well as all allopathic treatments, have the potential to create healing.

Be careful when working around the head as this is a very sensitive area.

Different names, same healing

There are many different names for healing, including "spiritual healing," "psychic healing" and "faith healing." However, these names can be rather confusing:

• **Spiritual healing** implies that spirits are involved, which can be an off-putting concept for some people.

• **Psychic healing** can sound equally scary to someone who is unnerved by the thought of psychic powers.

• **Faith healing** suggests that the healing will only work on people with sufficient faith, or with a particular belief.

• **Energy healing** is a better description of how healing works, because it acknowledges the essential role that energy plays in the process. It is a three-way process between the patient, the healer and the higher source to which the healer connects. Different healers have different names for this source, according to their own spiritual beliefs; they might refer to it as God, the Universe or the Source. Giving healing without linking to a higher source can sometimes lead to fatigue in the healer.

WHO IS DOING THE HEALING?

Most energy healers believe that their healing ability is channeled through them from a higher power to their patients. They believe that they act as a conduit, not as the source of healing itself. Some healers disagree with this, believing that they are the actual source of the healing power. However, the role of the patient is also essential, because energy healing nudges the patient's body into healing itself.

Psychic surgery

Just as there are many forms of healing, so there are many forms of psychic surgery. The most dramatic examples of this type of healing are practiced primarily in Brazil and the Philippines, where healers apparently perform surgery on a patient's body without using any medical equipment or anaesthetic. They frequently remove

Edivaldo Silva is one of Brazil's most celebrated psychic surgeons.

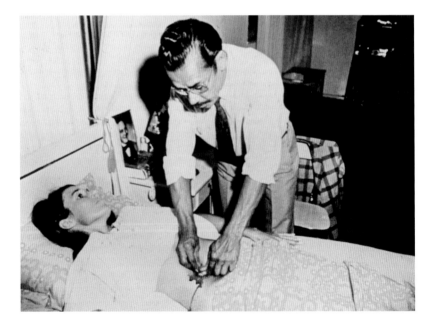

large lumps of tissue, such as tumors and gallstones, from their patients' bodies, complete with some of the attendant gore. Many patients have been cured by these methods.

IN THE PHILIPPINES AND BRAZIL

The most common description of a psychic operation defies the classic Western concept of a medical procedure. The surgeon slips his hands (or a table knife) into the body of the patient without using an anaesthetic, removes or heals whatever is troubling that patient, and then closes up the wound without using stitches or plasters. The wounds heal completely within a few days—rather than weeks, as is normal in the West. These operations are often messy and bloody, in complete contrast to ordinary energy healing as practiced in the West.

Any form of healing attracts sceptics, but psychic surgery receives the most criticism. It is an easy target for debunkers of psychic phenomena, who cite the innumerable cases of fraud and then use these to discredit the entire practice. However, the fact that many

Westerners don't understand genuine psychic surgery, or dare not believe in it because it challenges everything they've been taught, does not automatically mean it is fraudulent.

IN THE WEST

There are some renowned psychic surgeons practicing in the West, too. One of the best-known is Stephen Turoff, who works in Britain. Not a trained surgeon, he channels the instructions of a team of doctors in the spirit world. These doctors are led by Dr. Joseph Khan, an Austrian who died in the early 1900s.

The discarnate entity called Dr. William Lang works with George Chapman, a former fireman, and his son Michael. Dr. Lang even gives consultations to his patients while George or Michael Chapman is in a trance. When he was alive, Dr. Lang worked as a noted eye surgeon at Moorfields Eye Hospital in London. Occasionally, working through one of the Chapmans, Dr. Lang has treated patients whom he first met when he worked at Moorfields. These patients recognize him.

The work of Edgar Cayce

Edgar Cayce's workload eventually became so demanding that he died from a stroke in 1945.

One of the most remarkable characters in the history of psychic healing is Edgar Cayce, often called "the sleeping prophet." Cayce's story is so extraordinary that his detractors believe his healing work must have involved trickery, suggestibility, a desire for financial gain and every other racket they can imagine.

Yet Cayce was rigorous in testing his own work, and many of his treatments are still being used to cure patients today. What is more, he usually refused to accept any form of payment for his work.

Edgar Cayce was born on a farm in Kentucky in 1877. He was a poor student at school and seemed ordinary, with one notable exception: he had strong psychic gifts. When struggling with his lessons, he discovered that he could absorb all the information in a school book if he slept with it under his pillow.

TRANCE READINGS

This was remarkable enough, but as a young man Cayce developed the ability to put himself into a trance and diagnose a cure for a patient's health problems. When awake, he had virtually no medical knowledge; in a trance, his knowledge was boundless. Cayce quickly became celebrated as someone who could cure patients of seemingly intractable, and often life-threatening, conditions. At first he worked in close physical proximity to the patient, but he soon realized that he could heal anyone in the world—all he needed was the patient's name and address.

Many of Cayce's treatments followed a pattern. He often recommended osteopathy, describing exactly which bones in the spine were to be manipulated. Another favorite treatment was applying poultices steeped in warm castor oil to the affected part of the body. Cayce also suggested exercise programs and changes of diet, as well as medical treatments. He would often prescribe medicines that were considered quaintly old-fashioned, but which cured everything from mild ailments to serious conditions. Although many of his treatments were considered wacky, or too mild to do any good, in the vast majority of cases they worked. He set up his own research organization, the Association for Research and Enlightenment (ARE), to investigate the success of his readings. He was judged to have a success rate of more than ninety percent.

One of the most curious aspects of Cayce's abilities was that he was a strongly religious man, whose Christian beliefs bordered on fundamentalism and were sometimes at odds with what he said in a trance. For instance, he often spoke of the Akashic Records (believed to exist on the astral plane and to contain the entire life records of everyone who has lived) when in a trance, although he was puzzled by the very idea of them when he was awake.

THE UNIVERSAL MIND

What did Cayce himself think about his powers? He was aware that, while in trance, his mind seemed able to do two things at once: he could give a reading for someone while also having a personal dream. Sometimes he would pick up a person's thoughts while giving the reading and would respond to what she was thinking.

Cayce believed that his powers came from what he called the universal or soul mind, which bears a strong resemblance to Carl Jung's concept of the collective unconscious. So when Cayce went into a trance, he was able to merge with the whole of life and access any information he needed through the Akashic Records.

Giving healing

When you start to develop your healing abilities, you will want to practice them on other people. But no matter how strong your urge to heal others, there are some important guidelines to follow (see below).

Healing guidelines

These apply to every healing session, whoever you are healing. They are all common sense, but it is important to remember them:

• Don't give someone a medical diagnosis unless you are medically qualified and have been specifically asked to do so.

• Never tell someone that he is now cured and can stop taking his medication or will not be needing an operation.

• Never dissuade someone from seeking medical advice, or promise him that you will be able to heal his problem.

• Don't frighten your patient by saying that you can see all sorts of horrible things in his aura.

• Always ask the person for his permission to give him healing, even if you do this mentally. Don't force healing on someone without his knowledge.

SETTING THE SCENE

When healing another person, do so in a soothing, calm atmosphere. Provide a comfortable chair for your patient (make sure that both her feet are in contact with the floor, even if she has to rest her feet on a cushion) or ask her to lie down on a bed or massage table.

You might wish to play some gentle background music, but do check with your patient first in case she dislikes this for some reason. Equally you might want to burn a candle or some incense, but check whether your patient is happy about this. Make sure that you yourself don't smell strongly of anything (even if it's only your favorite scent), because this can distract the patient.

Ensure that you won't be disturbed—whether by someone coming into the room or by a ringing telephone. Don't forget to ask your patient to switch off her mobile phone before you begin the healing session.

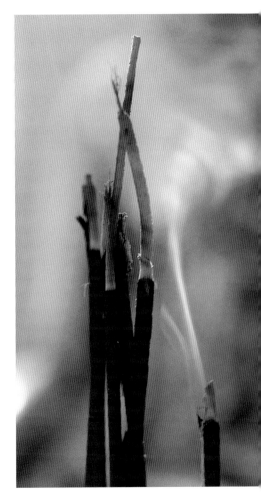

Only burn incense during healing if you've checked that your patient likes the smell.

HEALING ANOTHER PERSON

The simplicity of this healing procedure is belied by its effectiveness. Having said that, don't expect instant miracles: healing often takes time to work. All you need do is maintain your connection to the source of the healing energy, and channel it through you and out through your hands. Let the healing energy—and the patient's body—do the rest.

1 Invite your patient to sit or lie down as appropriate, then check that he's comfortable. Tell him he can keep his eyes open or closed, and that you will inform him when the healing has finished. Ask if he minds you touching his shoulders and feet during the healing. If he does, you can rest your hands just above his body, which will be equally effective.

2 Stand to one side of your patient and mentally ground and balance yourself (see pages 24–25). Imagine that you're bathing in a shower of golden light, to clean your aura. Then picture a beam of light being sent from the highest source of healing that you can think of and entering the crown of your head.

3 Gently place your hands on the patient's shoulders and imagine that you are both surrounded by a protective cloak of light.

4 You are now ready to begin the healing session. You can either work on each chakra in turn, starting with the base chakra and moving up to the crown chakra (see pages 66–79), or simply heal whichever area of the patient's aura you feel is appropriate (see pages 92–95). Check occasionally that he's comfortable.

5 When you have finished, tell the patient you are going to place your hands on his feet—otherwise you might give him a shock. Imagine that roots are growing down into the earth from the soles of his feet (this is to ground him). Mentally give thanks for the healing energy.

6 Move away from him and imagine that you're being bathed in a shower of light. Then ground yourself again.

7 Gently tell your patient that the healing has finished. Invite him to comment on what he experienced, and tell him your own experiences, where appropriate.

Healing techniques

When you are conducting a healing, whether it's for you or someone else, you are manipulating the energy contained within the aura. After a short time this change in the energetic structure of the aura will be reflected in the physical body, as an ailment starts to improve. That is because problems always manifest first in the aura and, if not resolved, eventually affect the physical body. Therefore you work on the aura to clear the physical problem.

Here are some simple healing techniques that you can use. As you become more practiced at healing, you may instinctively develop other approaches that you feel are suitable at the time. Some will become favorite techniques, while others you will only use on rare occasions. What is important is that you feel comfortable with what you're doing, and confident that you are indeed carrying out healing. As you work, keep checking that your patient is comfortable, especially when working around her head as this can be a very sensitive area.

SMOOTHING THE AURA
This is one of the simplest, but most effective, healing techniques that you

You can heal yourself by working on the aura around the affected area of your body.

While giving healing it's a good idea to check the energy of each chakra.

can use. It is especially good when a section of aura feels lumpy, hot or discordant in some way. For instance, you could use it to heal a wasp sting or a cut. Hold your palm about 2 in. (5 cm) away from the affected part of the body and use it to smooth the aura. Move your hand in long, steady strokes until the aura feels better. As you work, know that your actions are having a beneficial effect.

FOCUSING ON THE AURA

This is another simple technique with impressive results. It is extremely beneficial when you want to calm an area of the aura. The person receiving the healing may feel a strong sensation of comforting warmth from your hand, even though it isn't in contact with her body. Hold your palm about 2 in. (5 cm) above the area that you want to heal and keep it there. Imagine that healing energy is flowing down through the crown of your head and out through your palm into the person's aura.

BREAKING UP ITS ENERGY

If a section of the aura feels heavy, as though the energy is blocked or

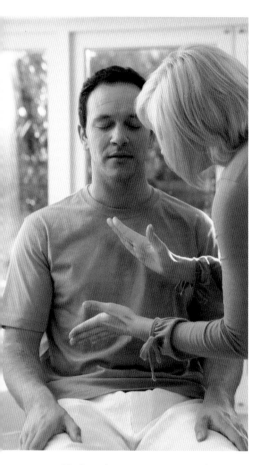

It's always best to warn your patient before you start to make a noise, such as clapping.

sluggish, you need to get that energy moving again by breaking it up. You can do this by clapping your hands, rubbing them together or flicking your fingers through the aura—whatever feels most suitable. Keep alternating between breaking up the energy and testing to see how it feels. If in doubt, ask your patient for feedback.

REMOVING STUCK ENERGY

Sometimes the best way to work with stuck energy, which feels heavy or blocked, is to pull it out of the aura with your hands and deposit it in an imaginary bucket. This is tremendously effective, especially if you bathe the affected area in golden light after you have finished working on it.

As you work, you may get a mental impression of what you are removing. For example, you might sense that your patient's stomach is filled with stones, which you remove and place in your imaginary container, or it may seem to you that a sprained wrist contains long needles that must be carefully extracted. Trust your intuition, rather than your logical mind, and gently remove these energetic foreign bodies. Continue until the aura feels clear. Ask for the energy in the bucket to be removed and disposed of carefully.

LEAVING YOUR HAND IN THE AURA

Problems in the aura aren't always solved in one healing session. If you are healing a long-term ailment, you can mentally leave your hands in the

Don't worry about whether your healing techniques seem strange to your patient.

person's aura at the end of the session. Simply place your hands above the affected part of the body and then mentally leave them there. The effect of the healing from your hands will continue, even though you have physically removed them.

Examining your body psychically

There are several ways to examine your own body psychically. Your chosen method depends on the way your mind works. Are you better at sensing energy with your hands, seeing it in your mind's eye or actually viewing it in your aura? Choose the process that works best for you, and believe that what you are doing is really happening. Remember, energy follows thought.

SCANNING YOUR BODY

In this exercise, you run your hands slowly over your aura, sensing its energy. You are looking for hot or cold spots, heavy areas or any other sensations that feel strange, uncomfortable or unusual.

1 Stand with both feet hip-width apart. Ground and balance yourself (see pages 24–25).

2 Using your dominant hand (the one you write with), start to move it over your body, always holding it a short distance away from your skin. Pay careful attention to the sensations in your hand.

3 Work systematically down your non-dominant arm, then switch hands and scan your dominant arm. Now scan the front of your trunk and each leg, using your dominant hand where possible. Don't forget to scan the soles of your feet.

4 It's more difficult to scan your back, especially if you aren't very flexible. Stretch your arms so that you can feel as much of your back as possible.

5 Whenever you find a problem area, use whichever healing techniques (see pages 138–141) seem appropriate. As you work, know that you are healing your body.

6 When you have finished, give thanks for being able to feel the energy, and ground yourself once again.

SCANNING YOUR CHAKRAS

This is a very good exercise if you want to tune into the state of your chakras. It teaches you to use the palm of your hand to dowse the energy of each chakra and tune into the way it is spinning. The more you practice this exercise, the more sensitive your palms will become. Healthy chakras spin round in circles. However, very often our chakras can become sluggish and develop an eccentric spin that needs to be adjusted. You can do this by mentally altering the spin until it is smooth and circular.

1 Sit in a comfortable chair or stand with your legs hip-width apart. Ground and balance yourself, as before.

2 Using your dominant hand, hold your palm close to your base chakra (see pages 66–67), between your legs, but without actually touching your body. Register the sensations you receive. Don't worry if you can't feel anything: simply imagine that your base chakra is spinning well.

3 Move your hand up to your sacral chakra (see pages 68–69) and repeat the exercise. Tune into the sensations that you're feeling in your palm, and adjust the spin of the chakra if necessary.

4 Work up your body until you have reached your throat chakra (see pages 74–75). The aura around your head is very sensitive, so at this point you may find it more comfortable to move your hand slightly further away from your body.

5 When you reach your crown chakra (see pages 78–79), use both hands to sense it. Hold them above each side of your head and tune into the spin of your crown chakra. You may feel it spinning around between your hands.

6 Whenever you find a problem area, use whichever healing techniques (see pages 138–141) seem appropriate. As you work, know that you are healing your body.

7 When you have finished, give thanks for the healing energy and ground yourself once again.

USING YOUR MIND'S EYE

It may be that you are happiest using your mind's eye, rather than your hands, to scan your body. This is just as effective as any other method, but you must learn to trust the impressions you receive.

1 Sit comfortably with both feet flat on the floor, and ground and balance yourself, as before. You can work with your eyes open or closed, according to what feels most natural for you.

2 Try one of two methods of examining your body with your mind's eye. The first is to move your attention around each area of your body in turn, working slowly. How does it feel? Are you aware of any tense, painful or uncomfortable areas? The second is to imagine that you can see your own body energetically, so that you're looking at its aura and chakras. How does it look? Are the chakras spinning well? Is your aura clear or does it contain areas of blocked energy?

3 Whenever you find a problem area, use whichever healing techniques (see pages 138–141) seem appropriate. As you work, know that you are healing your body.

4 When you have finished the exercise, give thanks and ground yourself once again.

OBSERVING YOUR AURA

In this exercise you are actually looking at your aura. You will find this easiest if you work in front of a full-length mirror, with access to another mirror that you can move around so that you can see your back.

1 Stand in front of the mirror with both feet hip-width apart and your knees slightly bent, then ground and balance yourself, as before.

2 Start by looking at the aura around your head. Remember to let your eyes relax so that you aren't looking directly at the space around your head—you're looking beyond it.

3 Now look at the aura around each area of your body in turn. What does it look like? Can you see any dark areas of blocked energy, or areas where your aura is thinner and less strong? Check that your aura extends down your legs and tucks under your feet, and that there are no holes or tears in your aura.

4 Whenever you find a problem area, use whichever healing techniques (see pages 138–141) seem appropriate. As you work, know that you are healing your body.

5 When you have finished, give thanks and ground yourself again.

Absent healing

All healing involves energy, so it is equally effective whether it is given when the healer and patient are in the same room (often known as "contact healing") or when they are far apart (known as "absent healing"). This can be a difficult concept to grasp at first, especially if the only sort of healing you have experienced involves consulting your doctor face-to-face. How can a healer send you healing when she is a long way away?

Energy follows thought, so a healer has only to think of the person to whom she wants to send healing for it to reach him. The more frequently the healer sends out that energy, the stronger the connection between her and the patient will become.

Absent healing is extremely effective. In fact, many healers find that absent healing has an even greater impact on the patient than contact healing. It is also very convenient, because the healer can send healing to her patient at any time, wherever she happens to be.

When giving absent healing, always imagine that your patient is in vibrant good health.

You can even send someone absent healing when you're talking to him on the phone.

The ethics of absent healing

The ethical guidelines given for contact healing (see pages 134–135) apply equally to absent healing. However, the most important rule is that healers shouldn't send healing to people without their permission. This can be hard to understand and often seems rather contrary. If you are a healer and you see someone in distress, surely it's natural to send him healing? Well, no. You are interfering in his free will if you send him healing without his permission. What you could do instead is to send him love or ask God (or the healing angels) to help him.

Sometimes you may want to send healing to someone you love, yet for some reason you can't ask her permission. In this case, you can mentally ask her higher self if she would like to receive healing. You will always get an answer, and you must honor it if it's a loud "No."

Sending absent healing

There are several ways in which you can send absent healing. As with contact healing, you need to find which system works best for you. It might be different from that used by the other healers you know, but that doesn't matter, provided you follow the guidelines for ethical healing outlined on page 149.

CREATING A SANCTUARY

You can send out healing energy at any time, in any place, but at first you might prefer to create a peaceful sanctuary in which to practice absent healing. This increases its spiritual qualities and will help put you in a more relaxed mood, so that the healing can flow easily without you trying too hard. Healing flows best when you are relaxed, not when you're trying to force it out of yourself and into another person.

Even a small corner of a room can be turned into a sanctuary. You might like to use it for meditation as well, so that it builds up a powerful energy. Perhaps you could light a candle when you do your healing, or you might like to create a small altar or put up inspirational pictures. The choice is yours.

TUNING IN AT THE SAME TIME

Many healers like to send absent healing at the same time every day. This creates a ritual so that it builds in power, and they are less likely to forget to do it. You only need spend a few minutes sending healing, although you can always spend longer if you wish.

However, this doesn't mean that you can only send healing when you are in your sanctuary. You can send it when you are on a bus or walking down the road. It is the intention that is important, not the setting. Always try to send the healing with love, compassion and understanding.

There is no need to make your altar conspicuous if you don't want to draw attention to it.

SENDING HEALING TO ONE PERSON

1 Choose a time when you won't be disturbed, and sit comfortably with both feet flat on the floor. Prepare by grounding yourself (see pages 24–25), then imagine that you're bathing in a shower of golden light, and picture a beam of healing light entering the crown of your head.

2 Close your eyes and, either mentally or out loud, ask for healing to be sent to your patient. Say his name, as this sets up a powerful energetic force between you.

3 Imagine his entire body being bathed in healing light. Alternatively, concentrate on the area of his body that needs healing. Imagine yourself working on it just as you would if you were in the same room.

4 See the physical problem fading away, to be replaced by radiant health. Avoid negative words. For instance, rather than saying, "Please cure John Smith's cancer," you should say, "Please send perfect health to John Smith."

5 When you feel ready to stop, mentally enclose your patient in a bubble of golden light, then picture him walking away from you through an archway. This is to break the psychic tie between you.

6 Mentally have a shower in golden light, then ground yourself again. Give thanks for the healing.

7 Open your eyes and stretch your arms and legs to bring yourself fully back into your body.

SENDING HEALING TO A GROUP

As you become more practiced as a healer, you will invariably collect a list of people to whom you want to send absent healing. There are two ways in which you can do this, but for either method follow the basic framework described opposite, including preparing yourself to send healing.

For the first method, say each person's name in turn. As you say each name, picture that person being bathed in healing light. See him happy, strong and healthy; then see him walk away through the archway. Now say the name of the next person on your list, and repeat the procedure. Continue until you have given healing to each person in the group. Then end the healing in the usual way.

The second method is especially useful if many people want to be healed and you don't have the time to go through them individually. Write all their names on a sheet of paper, then place your hand on the paper and ask for them all to be sent healing. Know that this is happening.

Giving healing to animals

Animals respond to healing just as readily as humans. In many cases, animals enjoy and accept healing much more readily than humans, so they make excellent patients. They don't get caught up in questions about whether they're responding to the placebo effect or whether they would have got better anyway without the healing. In the vast majority of cases, they simply settle down to soak up the healing energy.

WHY ANIMALS NEED HEALING
Animals become ill, just like humans. They can also become tired, despondent, depressed, anxious, nervy, bored or emotionally dependent and, if left untreated, these conditions can eventually turn into a physical ailment. One of the best ways to ensure that

You should always seek a vet's help if an animal is suffering in any way.

your pet remains in good health—both physically and mentally—is to give her a little hands-on healing every day. You can do this very simply with small pets, such as cats and dogs: place one hand on the animal's stomach and the other on the back of her neck, and feel the healing energy flowing through your hands. Adapt the procedure for larger animals such as horses by placing your hands wherever you can reach or feel most comfortable.

A point of law

In most cases, animals are protected under the law of the country in which they reside, because they are entirely dependent on the goodwill of humans for their medical care and support. Therefore there are strict laws governing the care and healing of animals, although these may differ from one country to the next. For instance, owners of pets in the UK need a referral from their vet before taking an animal to a homeopathic vet or a pet healer. In the US, the law varies from state to state.

However, there is nothing to stop you giving hands-on healing to your own pets, provided that you also consult your vet about the problems the animal is experiencing. There are many examples of pets that have responded on an almost miraculous level to healing from their owners. They also respond well to homeopathy and flower remedies, among many other complementary treatments. You will soon discover which treatments most suit your own pets.

Psychic tools

What are psychic tools?

Put simply, a psychic tool is an object or practice that enables you to make a strong connection with your intuition and with the spirit realms. It might help to think of a psychic tool as a bridge between every day reality and spirit. Actually, the tool itself—whether it's a crystal, a pendulum or anything else that you wish to use—is not psychic. It is merely the facilitator of your own psychic abilities, so it enables them to flow. You might imagine that the pendulum or crystal is doing all the work, but in reality it is you. Your chosen tool is simply showing you the results of your own psychic abilities.

As you progress and become more confident about using and trusting your psychic powers, you may find that you can dispense with

some of the psychic tools mentioned in this section. For instance, the chakras located in your hands (see pages 64–65) might become so sensitive that you won't always need to use your pendulum to sense energy or to dowse whether a particular foodstuff is right for you.

FINDING WHAT SUITS YOU

It's a good idea to experiment with the different psychic tools until you find the ones with which you're most comfortable. You will inevitably have a greater affinity with some than with others, or find that you have a gift for

Crystals are very effective psychic tools if you have an affinity for them.

using your psychic abilities in a particular way. What you must remember is that no psychic tool is better than another. Psychic work is not competitive (although some people might make it so), nor is there any pecking order involved, making some psychic tools more special or enlightened than others. Each tool has its own qualities and gifts. It is simply a question of finding which ones suit you best, and then developing your relationship with them so that you can use them with confidence, enjoyment and success.

Tarot cards accurately reflect the dynamics of a situation and provide insight into it.

Crystals

Crystals are immensely effective. They transmit great power, which you can train yourself to detect with your hands or to see in your mind's eye. For instance, if you pass your palm over an amethyst you will feel a cool breeze radiating from it.

Crystals are created by geophysical forces within the earth whenever its crust is put under enormous stress. They hold the memory of the tremendous forces that were involved, which is why they have such strength.

BUYING CRYSTALS

You may already own crystals without realizing it. For instance, you may have jewelry decorated with diamonds, sapphires, emeralds, rubies or amethysts. This is an excellent way to work with crystals, and many others are also available as jewelry. Alternatively, you can buy crystals in different forms, such

A single terminated crystal is very versatile but you must choose one that you like.

as polished stones, geodes (hollow rocks lined with crystals) or in their raw state.

You might imagine that the bigger the crystal, the stronger its power, but this is not true. Small crystals are just as powerful and have the bonus of being easily portable, so that you can carry them around with you if you wish.

Many shops sell crystals and it is worth visiting a few of them to see what is available. Get a feel for the different crystals, and don't be afraid to ask if you're looking for a crystal that will perform a specific function, such as giving you psychic protection. You can also buy crystals over the Internet, but make sure you can return them if you don't like their energy.

It's essential to choose the right crystal: you must be comfortable with it and feel attracted to it. Although you will think that you are choosing the crystal, in reality it's more a case of the crystal choosing you. For instance, you might notice one that seems to shine more brightly or look more friendly

The size of a crystal bears no relation to its effectiveness, so big isn't better.

than the others; or, as you sift through a bowl of crystals, one might apparently jump into your hand—this is the crystal for you.

If you want a crystal for a particular chakra (see pages 64–81), you should choose a crystal of the corresponding color.

CARING FOR YOUR CRYSTALS

Crystals absorb the energy around them, which is why they're so good for healing, so it's very important to clean them when you get them home because they will have soaked up energy from the shop and the people who have handled them. As you work with them, they will also absorb your own energies, so periodically you will need to clean them.

Some crystals can be washed in running water, but others will dissolve when given this treatment. If you aren't sure how to take care of your crystals, you might prefer to cleanse them all by leaving them in moonlight, or by imagining that they are being bathed in white light.

Check that you can wash your crystals in water as some will be permanently damaged by such treatment.

Dedicating your crystal

Before you begin to work with your crystal, you must tell it what you want it to do. After cleaning it, hold it and send it loving thoughts. Now imagine light streaming into it from your third eye or brow chakra (see pages 76–77). When you are ready, say aloud, "I dedicate this crystal to [state whatever is appropriate]. May it work for the highest good of all concerned." Repeat this dedication every day and whenever you work with the crystal, in order to increase its power.

CRYSTAL QUALITIES

Different crystals are associated with different colors and qualities, and with specific healing attributes. Below are descriptions of some of the most popular healing crystals.

Clear quartz

This is a good all-around crystal because it contains every color of the spectrum. It is highly effective for healing because it is such an excellent conductor of energy and is suitable for all chakras. You can use a single-terminated clear quartz to hook out areas of stagnant energy in your aura.

Carnelian

Carnelian is found in red, pink, orange and brown forms. It is very good at grounding you and is also an excellent healer. During difficult times it will give you courage. Carnelian is a powerful stone for healing the base chakra.

Citrine

As its color suggests, this orange crystal is a great energizer. It is cheering and joyful, and encourages optimism. Citrine is also an excellent crystal for attracting prosperity on all levels. It is a powerful stone for use in healing, especially when working on the solar-plexus, heart and crown chakras.

Black tourmaline

This handsome stone is excellent at providing grounding and psychic protection. Carry it in your pocket if you are having problems with the people around you, because it will shield you from their negative thoughts. It is an excellent crystal for use with the base chakra.

Amethyst

Amethyst was traditionally worn to prevent drunkenness, and it is excellent at instilling a sense of calm and peace.

Black tourmaline

Clear quartz

Carnelian

Citrine

It is a beneficial stone to use for healing, especially when you feel anxious and can't sleep. Amethyst is a good crystal for use with the throat chakra.

Lapis lazuli

This beautiful blue stone increases psychic abilities and helps you to make contact with your spirit guides through your brow chakra. It is also linked to the throat chakra and is therefore excellent at encouraging all forms of communication.

Rose quartz

This is a very pretty crystal whose primary function is to promote unconditional love and compassion. It is therefore linked to the heart chakra and heals heart-related problems, whether physical or emotional. Rose quartz is beneficial in times of crisis because it instills a sense of calm.

Topaz

Topaz is available in many colors, including yellow, brown, blue and green. It's a useful stone for healing digestive disorders, and is also excellent for improving wisdom and intuition. In addition, you can use it to strengthen your affirmations and to manifest your goals. In healing, it is attuned to the sacral chakra.

Calcite

You can buy this crystal in a variety of colors, from red to green. It is a highly effective purifier, whether of the atmosphere in a room or a mental or emotional state. It also helps you to turn ideas into reality, so is excellent in prosperity work and creative visualization, and is also effective at increasing your psychic skills. Orange calcite has a great affinity with the sacral chakra.

Amethyst

Topaz

Rose quartz

Lapis lazuli

Calcite

Dowsing

Dowsing, also known as "divining," is one of the oldest skills known to humans. It is very simple, but remarkably effective. Dowsing is used by water companies to detect leaks in pipes, by oil companies to locate new reserves of oil and other mineral deposits, and by chicken-sexers who process chicks (using the swing of the pendulum to determine their sex) at a remarkable speed. It can also be used in everyday life to track down missing items or to receive answers to questions. In fact, dowsing is immensely versatile. You can even use it to discover which foods are good for you.

HOW DO YOU DOWSE?

Dowsing is easily practiced with a pendulum, although you can also use a pair of dowsing rods. The dowsing instrument reacts in a previously specified way when it locates whatever it is searching for. A pendulum, for example, might start to rotate in a clockwise direction and a pair of dowsing rods might jerk upwards or cross each other. If you have very sensitive chakras in your hands (see pages 64–65), you may find that you are able to dispense with a pendulum or dowsing rods completely and use your hands instead.

USING A PENDULUM

The pendulum can be made from brass, wood or crystal, and is suspended from a piece of cord or string. It doesn't matter what the pendulum is made from, provided it is symmetrical (so as not to distort the swing) and heavy enough to oscillate properly and gain a good momentum. You need a long enough piece of cord or string to enable the pendulum to move easily. As with the other psychic tools, choose the pendulum that feels right for you.

You must spend time training your pendulum so it always gives you accurate responses.

TRAINING YOUR PENDULUM

When you first start to use a pendulum you must train it to react in the way you want, so that you will know what it is telling you. You must therefore train it to give you "Yes," "No," "Silly question" and "Search" responses. The first two responses are self-evident, and "Search" will tell you that the pendulum is busily looking for whatever you have asked it to find. "Silly question" might seem unnecessary, but actually it's very helpful. You need to know when you have asked your pendulum a question that it can't answer, otherwise you might misinterpret its response. For instance, if you ask the pendulum a multiple-choice question, such as "Is coffee or tea better for me?," it can't answer and will respond with "Silly question." You will have to break your question into two halves in order to get a proper answer from the pendulum. Sometimes you will get "Silly question" for reasons that you can't fathom. When this happens, it is either because the pendulum is not cooperating with you (in which case you need to keep working with it until it does) or because the question has already been answered in ways that you don't yet realize.

1 **"Yes" response** Start by training your pendulum to give you the "Yes" response. Hold the cord lightly between your thumb and forefinger, then ask the pendulum to show you its "Yes" swing. You can either ask it out loud or mentally, then start to swing the pendulum. Watch its swing settle into a specific pattern, such as an even, clockwise rotation. Now repeat the exercise. Ideally, the pendulum will behave in the same way as before. If it doesn't, you must stop it and try again. It is very important to let the pendulum know that you're in charge. Continue this exercise until you always get the same movement for "Yes."

2 **"No" response** Now repeat the exercise, but ask for the "No" response. You use the same technique as for the "Yes" response, but you're looking for a different swing. For instance, if "Yes" is an even, clockwise swing, "No" might be an elliptical, counterclockwise swing. You need these two swings to be noticeably different so that you can tell which is which.

3 **"Search" and "Silly question" responses** Continue like this for the "Search" and "Silly question" responses. "Search" is often a wide swing, as though the pendulum is feeling for the desired object in space. "Silly question" is often an indeterminate, obscure swing.

4 When you have determined all four responses, you can begin to refine your pendulum techniques. Ask the pendulum to give you one response, such as "No," then ask it to change its swing to "Yes." The more you practice working with your pendulum like this, the better your rapport will be and the more effective the pendulum will become.

KEEPING A CLEAR MIND

Don't allow your thoughts to distract you while using your pendulum. If you're too emotionally involved in your question ("Does she love me?" would probably come into this category), you may affect its outcome, so it's important to keep your thoughts clear while waiting for the pendulum's response.

WORKING WITH YOUR PENDULUM

When you're completely comfortable with your pendulum, and vice versa, it's time to begin using it. The more you use it, the more practiced you will become. However, you must always run through its four responses (see pages 168–169) before you ask it a question, to check that they haven't changed since you last used it.

In addition to asking your pendulum questions about situations in which you're involved, you can also consult it on other matters. For instance, you could dowse the flower remedies that are most suitable for you on a particular day. If you're looking for a new home, you could dowse a map for the best location in which to search. One of the most useful dowsing techniques is to track down objects that you have mislaid. For example, if you have lost your contact lens case somewhere at home, you can stand in each doorway in turn and dowse to see if the case is somewhere in that room. This will help

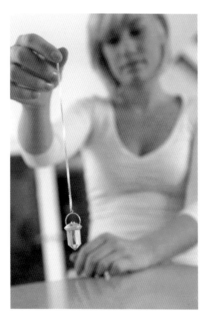

Pendulums come in many shapes and sizes. Choose the one you feel you can work with.

to narrow down the search. When you know which room contains the case, you can walk around it with the pendulum in "Search" mode until it switches to "Yes."

A pendulum is especially useful when you're searching for a lost object.

Flower remedies

The art of using flower remedies is thought to date back thousands of years, although they did not enjoy a revival until the 1930s, when a British doctor and bacteriologist began to explore the healing potential of flowers. He was Dr. Edward Bach, whose name is now known throughout the world because of the thirty-eight Bach Flower Remedies that he discovered.

Dr. Bach was looking for plants that would cure patients of whatever ailed them, and he knew he would prescribe the plants according to the patient's personality, rather than her symptoms. His body was so sensitive that he was able to discover the plants he needed purely by touching them and recording the effects they had on him.

DISTILLING THE ESSENCE

At first, Dr. Bach decided to gather the dew that collected on each plant's flowers at dawn, because he knew this would contain the essence of the plant, but he soon realized that it was an impractical task. Instead, he placed the flowers in a bowl of water and left them in the sun for a few hours. The water became charged with the essence of the plant and was very powerful.

When taking a flower remedy neat, try not to let the dropper touch your mouth or tongue.

Many flower remedies are equally effective whether taken neat or diluted in water.

Dr. Bach eventually discovered thirty-eight plants that together formed a perfect system for healing all emotional problems, from possessiveness to emotional detachment, timidity to over-exuberance. The remedies could be used in any combination and were prescribed according to the patient's emotional state at the time of the consultation. The results were dramatic, with patients being cured of physical ailments.

OTHER SYSTEMS

Dr. Bach's remedies gradually grew in popularity and have since inspired other ranges of flower remedies and essences around the world. In Australia, Ian White spent many years researching plants from the Australian bush, after first receiving information about them while sitting regularly in a healing circle. There are now fifty Australian Bush Flower Essences, as well as combination essences that are designed for specific purposes, such as clearing emotional baggage or creating abundance.

HOW DO FLOWER REMEDIES WORK?

At first it can be difficult to appreciate how a small brown bottle containing a highly diluted solution of flower-impregnated water can possibly have such a strong impact on someone, even to the extent of healing physical problems. Flower remedies work energetically and vibrate at a very high rate, so they quickly have a positive impact on our auras. You may notice this if you take flower remedies yourself: the emotion that you want to treat often falls away—as though it has been washed away—when you take the remedy or rub it on your skin. Even thinking about the remedy may help.

HOW DO YOU TAKE THEM?

There are two main ways to use flower remedies. The first is to ingest them, either by dropping them directly on to your tongue or by mixing them with a drink, such as water or tea. The second is to rub them on your skin or drop them into your bath water.

Most remedies can be diluted further from the stock bottle in which they're sold, but you should always check the manufacturer's instructions. If you intend to take the remedy for several days, it is a good idea to prepare a treatment bottle, as this will make the remedy go further. For this, you fill a 1 fl. oz. (25 ml) dropper bottle with fresh spring water, then add the recommended number of drops of your chosen remedy. Take four drops from your stock bottle as often as you wish, and not less than four times a day, until you either feel you no longer need the remedy or you have emptied the bottle and need to refill it.

Left: Put a flower remedy in your bathwater if you don't want to ingest the alcohol in which it is preserved.

CHOOSING YOUR REMEDIES

Several thousand flower remedies are now on sale throughout the world, in addition to gem elixirs, which are made by soaking crystals in water. Be prepared to experiment to find the ones that most suit you, according to your needs at the time.

You can create your own gem elixir by leaving a crystal to soak in a bowl of water.

Automatic writing

When you practice automatic writing, you are tuning into something beyond yourself. However, it's a moot point whether this is a spirit guide or your own unconscious. Only time will tell, when you're able to analyze the quality of what you have written.

WHAT IS AUTOMATIC WRITING?
Originally people practiced automatic writing by sitting with a pen or pencil poised over a sheaf of paper, waiting for the hand to start moving, apparently of its own accord. Another method was to use a planchette—a board mounted

True spirit communication

In rare cases, automatic writing involves the person's physical hand being guided by a spirit hand that has partially materialized. It is therefore the spirit who literally does the writing. However, this is most definitely the exception rather than the rule. One celebrated medium who was renowned for her automatic writing in the 1920s was Geraldine Cummins, who received communications alleged to emanate from Phillip the Evangelist, Cleophas, and F. W. H. Myers.

Another famous example of spirit communication is the book *Life in the World Unseen*. This was communicated in the early 1950s to its living author, Anthony Borgia, by Monsignor Robert Benson, who had already passed into the spirit realms and described in detail through automatic writing what he found there.

on castors with a receptacle in which a pencil fitted. The board would move freely over the paper as the sitter rested his hand on the pencil. The handwriting that was produced was always different from that of the sitter himself.

Today it is possible to practice automatic writing with a computer,

Your first attempts at automatic writing may not produce much, but they will improve with time.

although if you're going to do this, you should ideally be able to touch-type. Pausing to search for each key before striking it is bound to slow down the flow of the messages; it will also make you too conscious of what you're writing: the whole point of automatic writing is to let it flow through you. Being aware of what you are writing means that you may subconsciously block, control or alter it.

PRACTICING AUTOMATIC WRITING

As with every other psychic technique described in this book, you must make sure that you are grounded and balanced (see pages 24–25) and protected (see pages 104–109) before starting to practice automatic writing. You don't know who you will be communicating with, and you therefore need to protect yourself from any mischievous spirits who might enjoy misleading you. Automatic writing isn't something to do in an idle moment or for a laugh, because you are potentially dealing with a force that is much stronger than you. Be patient; your initial attempts may not produce much of interest, but they will improve with time.

1 Set aside some time when you won't be disturbed. Sit comfortably, with a pad of paper either resting on your knee or on a table in front of you. Make sure that your pen works or your pencil is sharp.

2 Ground, balance and protect yourself. You might wish to say a short prayer as well.

3 When you're ready, hold the pen or pencil over the paper and ask a spirit guide to draw near. Trust that this guide is with you, even if you can't feel anything, and begin to ask it some simple questions. For instance, you might like to ask its name and how it can help you. Write down each answer you receive, even if it only seems to be your imagination at work. Don't attempt to analyze or evaluate the answers you're receiving while you're writing. Stop after about 30 minutes.

4 Thank your guides for being with you and close down your chakras (see pages 188–189). You can now read what you have written. Although you will be very interested in the messages you have received, you should be discriminating about them. Spirit guides never issue orders or criticize you, so you should disregard any messages that do this.

Scrying and crystal balls

Humans have performed scrying for centuries. It's a very simple procedure, using nothing but a shiny surface. This acts as a backdrop to visions that come to you. You stare at the shiny surface, rather in the same way that you look at the area around a human body in order to perceive its aura (see pages 84–85).

Originally seers used a bowl of water, and this was certainly the practice in ancient Greece and Egypt. This is still a very effective method today.

Alternatively, you might prefer to follow the example of many alchemists and use a mirror, or you might enjoy working with a crystal ball.

SCRYING WITH WATER

Many psychics in China and the Middle East like to practice scrying with bowls of water. You can experiment with the size of bowl that works best for you, but its interior should not be decorated

It may take time to train yourself to scry, so don't expect instant results.

in any way because that might distort the images you see or suggest ideas to you. Ideally the bowl should be made of glass or metal to create a reflective surface. If you wish, you can scry with a glass of water, but you should only use the glass for scrying, so that it doesn't pick up other people's energies.

Use clean, fresh water, whether it's filtered or comes out of the tap. If you wish, you can bless it to change its energetic frequency. You can also increase its psychic charge by leaving the water in sunlight or moonlight before you use it.

SCRYING WITH A MIRROR

This was the method of John Dee, the Elizabethan astrologer and magician. However, he didn't use an ordinary mirror; it had a black back, instead of the customary silver one. You can make your own black mirror by carefully removing the glass from the frame and painting its back with several layers of matt black paint; replace the glass in its frame when the final layer of paint is completely dry.

When using a mirror for scrying, you mustn't look directly into it, because

When scrying with a mirror, you must position it so you can't see your reflection.

then you will be distracted by your own reflection. Sit to one side of it, so that you're looking at it from an angle. Cover up the mirror when it's not in use, to prevent it attracting too much energy from its surroundings.

SCRYING WITH A CRYSTAL BALL

Crystal balls come in many shapes and sizes, but it's important to use the one that suits you best. It can be large or small, clear, opaque or colored. You might be attracted to one with several flaws or you may prefer to use a crystal ball that is near-perfect.

When you get it home you must gently wash it in warm, soapy water and dry it with a soft cloth. Keep handling the crystal ball so that you impregnate it with your energies. Wrap it in a black or purple silk cloth when you aren't using it, and don't let other people touch it. The more you use it, the more receptive it will become.

HOW TO SCRY

Whether you're using a mirror, water or a crystal ball, the procedure for scrying is the same.

1 Choose a time when you won't be disturbed, and ground and balance yourself in the usual way (see pages 24–25).

2 Place the mirror, bowl or crystal ball on a dark surface. Dim the lights if working at night. Light a candle or nightlight, and leave it in a safe place out of your immediate vision so that it doesn't distract you.

3 Cup your hands around the mirror, bowl or crystal ball. Take several deep breaths and ask your spirit guide to help you with the reading. If you have a question, ask it now.

4 Gaze into the mirror, bowl or ball and keep your mind clear. Note any sensations or thoughts that come to you. Notice any images that you see in your mind's eye or which appear within your scrying tool.

5 Stop after about 20 minutes. Write down your experiences.

Forming a psychic circle

Psychic circles are also known as development circles, and are usually formed by people who want to develop their psychic abilities. They find that working as part of a group enhances their psychic energy and that they gain encouragement from assisting in one another's progress.

By their very nature, psychic circles attract sensitive people. It is important that everyone feels comfortable with one another, and ideally there shouldn't be any personality clashes, as these can disrupt the energy of the group and cause unhelpful distractions.

CREATING A FRAMEWORK

It's important to create a structured framework for the psychic circle so that everyone knows what they will be doing. You won't get anywhere if you have a vague format in which the group flits

Your psychic circle should meet at the same time each week.

from one topic to another. Instead, you need to plan ahead, so that every member of the circle knows what will be expected of them during the next meeting. In this way they can mentally start to prepare for the meeting, even if they do this at an unconscious level.

SETTING THE TONE

If you want to form a psychic circle, it's essential that you know what you're doing and that you treat the entire process with respect. It isn't a parlor game and you must proceed with caution and good intentions. If you are part of a psychic circle you will be attracting spirits to work with you, and will therefore want these spirits to be as enlightened and benign as possible. One of the best ways to encourage this is to make sure that the earthly participants are equally benign.

Although you might imagine that anyone who is interested in spiritual pursuits is automatically a pleasant person to have around, unfortunately that isn't always the case. If you're the one setting up the psychic circle, it's a good idea to interview each participant in advance so that you can get some idea of who to include and who to exclude. This might seem harsh, but groups can become very unbalanced as a result of one person wanting to be in the limelight all the time, being openly jealous of other people's psychic progress or operating a policy of divide and rule.

OPENING THE SITTING

Members of psychic circles may take a few weeks to settle into each other's energy, but after that they usually form very strong and loving bonds. This means that at the start of each meeting there is an opportunity for everyone to share their news and have a good gossip. Make sure this happens in another room—not the room in which you will all be working. This helps to separate the social aspect of the group from its serious side.

Create a set program (see page 188) for each meeting and always follow it. Even if you vary some of the items on the agenda (having informed everyone in advance), make sure that you always follow the same opening and closing rituals. Sit in a circle, close enough so that everyone can join hands if

necessary. It helps if everyone always sits in the same place, as this increases the sense of familiarity. Make sure everyone keeps both feet on the floor to establish a good grounding energy. If a participant is too short for her feet to touch the floor, she should rest them on a cushion.

You'll want to share your experiences with one another after each meeting.

Always open and close the circle with a prayer for psychic protection and to ask for the highest good for everyone present. When opening the circle, you can also invite everyone's spirit guides to draw near and join the circle (don't forget to thank them for their help at the end of the sitting).

CHOOSING A PROGRAM

It is up to you and your fellow members to decide what you want to do in your psychic circle. However, many groups have good results if they have a session of meditation (which can either be

silent or a guided visualization) before briefly discussing their experiences of it. You can then practice developing your psychic skills through such activities as psychometry (see pages 364–369), reading tarot cards (see pages 192–199) or some form of telepathy (see pages 374–377).

By now you will have built up a strong energy in the room and you may like to use it by practicing absent healing (see pages 150–153) at the end of the session. This is very effective if one person provides a guided visualization and each person in turn says the names of the people to whom they would like to send healing.

CLOSING DOWN THE CHAKRAS

It is essential for everyone to close down their chakras and ground themselves at the end of the session. If they don't do this, their chakras will still be wide open, making them very sensitive to what's going on around them and possibly leaving them vulnerable to

Psychometry is an excellent exercise for everyone in your psychic circle.

interference from discarnate entities.

An easy way to perform this closing down ceremony is for the leader to talk the rest of the group through the process. Everyone should close their eyes, then be guided to close down each chakra in turn, as though it were a flower shutting up its petals, starting with the crown chakra. After everyone has closed their base chakras, they should imagine themselves being showered with golden light, which will cleanse them of any residual psychic energy. They should then ground

If your feet can't touch the floor, rest them on a cushion so you are fully grounded.

themselves by imagining roots growing out of the soles of their feet and extending deep into the earth beneath them. When they know they are grounded, they can stretch, take a deep breath and gradually come back into awareness in the room.

At this point, everyone will be eager to discuss their experiences, while anyone who needs to leave quickly can do so without causing disruption.

Useful guidelines

Here are some suggestions for creating a strong circle that will be enjoyable and productive:

• The group should ideally meet on a regular basis: once a week is perfect. Everyone should do their best to attend the group each week, because people who drop in and out can disrupt the energy for everyone else.

• Make sure you always meet at the same place and at the same time, to establish a sense of continuity. Always using the same meeting place will encourage everyone's spirit guides to visit the group, because they will know this is a regular event.

• Every participant should pay a small amount of money each week to attend. This will help pay for the use of the rooms and for any additional expenses such as lighting, heating and refreshments. It also encourages members to take the group seriously.

• Appoint a leader of the group so that someone is in charge and is responsible for notifying everyone of any changes of plan from one week to the next. The leader can vary each week or month, so that everyone has a turn.

• Set a firm starting time and stick to it. You don't want anyone arriving late, because that will disrupt the atmosphere. You might decide that latecomers will have to wait for a suitable break in the proceedings before joining the group. You don't want someone dashing into the room and interrupting a group meditation.

• Avoid drinking alcohol before the sitting, because alcohol blurs perceptions and can attract unpleasant discarnate entities. And don't eat a heavy meal before the start of the group, or your body will be focused on your digestion, which could make you feel sleepy.

The tarot

Of the many systems of divination that are available to us, the tarot has retained a strong aura of mystery and secrecy. There is confusion about its origins, but it has been a very popular psychic tool since medieval times. It enjoyed increased popularity in the late 19th century, when the occult was being explored in all its forms, and is once again enjoying a revival.

WHAT DOES IT CONSIST OF?

The tarot is a deck of 78 cards, divided into two sections. These are the Major Arcana, which consists of 22 cards, and the Minor Arcana, which has 56 cards. The Major Arcana tells the story of our journey through life and some of the challenges that we encounter along the way. It begins with The Fool, who steps out into the world with childlike enthusiasm and innocence, and ends with The World, in which the wheel of

It's essential to work with a set of tarot cards that you like and which are easy to read.

karma (the law of cause and effect) has come full circle. The Major Arcana is always illustrated in ways that depict the cards' meanings.

The Minor Arcana is divided into four suits of 14 cards each. Each suit (Cups, Wands, Swords and Pentacles) consists of ten "pip" cards and four court cards. The Minor Arcana is believed to be the precursor of ordinary playing cards, of which there are 52 (playing cards only have three court cards in each suit), and there is certainly a strong link between their four suits. Cups are linked with Hearts, Wands with Clubs, Swords with Spades, and Pentacles with Diamonds. The Minor Arcana deals with the detailed situations we meet in life, such as making plans, coping with loss, feeling worried and achieving prosperity and fulfilment. Some tarot decks illustrate all the cards of the Minor Arcana, while others have plain "pip" cards and illustrated court cards.

WORKING WITH THE TAROT

It can be daunting when you first begin to work with the tarot because you must remember the meanings of all 78 cards. Some people use only the 22

In a tarot spread, the position of each card has a particular significance.

cards of the Major Arcana, but these don't give the comprehensive readings, rich in light and shade, that you experience when using the full deck.

The cards are laid out in special patterns known as spreads, and you then interpret the meaning of each card in relation to its position in the spread. You can read the cards for yourself or for another person. As you practice and gain in confidence, your readings will become richer and more intuitive.

Space permits only brief interpretations of each of the cards on the following pages. You can expand them yourself, either by using your intuition or by consulting an in-depth guidebook on the tarot.

The Major Arcana

Card	Meaning
The Fool	A fresh start, with optimism and childlike confidence.
The Magician	You have more power and versatility than you realize.
The High Priestess	Take note of your dreams, intuition and inner guidance. Trust your instincts.
The Empress	It is a time of creativity and abundance on any level.
The Emperor	Accept your authority and acknowledge your power.
The Hierophant	Adopt a conventional, traditional and careful approach to situations.
The Lovers	A strong emotional bond or a choice.
The Chariot	Face up to hard work and difficult experiences with will power.
Strength	Draw on your strength of purpose to beat the odds and triumph.
The Hermit	Some form of enlightenment, whether spiritual or educational.
Wheel of Fortune	A situation is about to alter. Nothing stays the same.
Justice	Behave in a fair and balanced manner. Don't pass judgment on others.

Card	Meaning
The Hanged Man	You need to view a situation from a different angle.
Death	A time of powerful psychological change and transformation.
Temperance	Bring more balance and moderation into your life.
The Devil	You feel enslaved by a situation, but you can break free from it.
The Tower	Sudden and dramatic events could cause loss of face and a change of fortune.
The Star	A dream could come true or a difficult situation will improve. Also, a recovery from illness.
The Moon	Things are not as they seem. There is a chance of deception and confusion.
The Sun	You will soon have more joy, creativity and fulfillment.
Judgment	Don't judge others too harshly. Some form of rebirth is possible.
The World	Worldly success, or the end of one cycle and the start of another.

The Minor Arcana: Wands

Card	Meaning
Ace	An exciting and enterprising new project, or a vacation or journey.
Two	Take stock of what you have achieved and what is still to be done.
Three	You have accomplished a great deal, but still have a long way to go.
Four	Celebrate your achievements after a period of hard work.
Five	Life is a struggle. This is a phase in which nothing goes to plan.
Six	Success—either through improved job prospects or increased status.
Seven	You need to fend off competition and rivalry by striving harder.
Eight	Life is very busy and things are happening quickly. Travel is likely.
Nine	You feel hemmed in by difficult circumstances. Don't take risks.
Ten	You're being weighed down by a heavy burden, but it can be lifted.
Page	A young, lively person or an exciting new enterprise or idea.
Knight	Some form of travel, or someone who is full of good ideas.
Queen	Someone who combines running a home with other interests.
King	Someone who is lively, enthusiastic and full of plans.

The Minor Arcana: Pentacles

Card	Meaning
Ace	A new business venture or anything else of material value.
Two	You need to juggle your finances or your time. Strive for balance.
Three	The division between the first stages of a project and the next step.
Four	Financial security, but a reluctance to take risks or escape from a rut.
Five	Don't be so caught up in problems that you ignore what's around you.
Six	You will soon either be giving or receiving money.
Seven	Are you making the best use of your skills and gifts?
Eight	A time of apprenticeship. Discover a new talent within yourself.
Nine	Triumph and pride in your achievements. A possible house move.
Ten	Completion, abundance, success and a happy family life.
Page	A reliable young person, or the receipt of a small amount of money.
Knight	A situation that has become bogged down. A cautious person.
Queen	Someone who is successful in business and a hard worker.
King	Someone who has material prosperity.

The Minor Arcana: Swords

Card	Meaning
Ace	A new idea that will be engrossing. A difficult decision or worry.
Two	An inability to make progress through fear of looking at what's wrong.
Three	A bleak time, often connected with betrayal, defection or deceit.
Four	A well-deserved rest after a period of hard work or illness.
Five	The need to accept your limitations and possibly to lose face.
Six	Difficult times will soon be over. Sometimes a change of location.
Seven	Sharpen your tactics and use your intelligence.
Eight	Fear is preventing you breaking free from your current situation.
Nine	Worries are hanging over you, but aren't as bad as they seem.
Ten	A difficult end to a cycle, leading to more positive times.
Page	Read the small print in agreements carefully. A clever young person.
Knight	A situation that starts quickly, gallops along and ends just as fast.
Queen	Valuable lessons learned through adversity.
King	The need to consult an expert.

The Minor Arcana: Cups

Card	Meaning
Ace	The start of a happy relationship or union, such as a love affair.
Two	A successful contract will soon be agreed. An amicable partnership.
Three	Happy friendship, or the relief that follows the resolution of a problem.
Four	An inability to appreciate everything that life has to offer.
Five	Something has ended in sorrow, but something has been salvaged.
Six	The past. Either something is revived or someone is being too nostalgic.
Seven	You will be offered several opportunities, but you should choose wisely.
Eight	An era in a relationship has ended and it is time to move on.
Nine	Happiness, stability and satisfaction. An ambition may soon be realized.
Ten	A marvelous achievement that brings you emotional satisfaction.
Page	A young, creative person or the start of a creative or spiritual enterprise.
Knight	An opportunity with creative, spiritual or emotional overtones.
Queen	Someone who is compassionate and possibly psychic.
King	Someone who has authority, but struggles to show emotions.

I Ching

This ancient Chinese form of divination is remarkably informative, accurate and helpful. Its name is translated as the Book of Changes, because it reflects the many changes that happen to us through our lives. A traditional I Ching reading is much more complicated than the interpretations listed here, but it is beyond the scope of this book to give them in more detail. However, several I Ching books are available, ranging from the complex and detailed to the very simple.

When consulting the I Ching, you ask a question and then throw three coins six times. Each time you throw the coins, you create a line of a hexagram (a group of six broken or unbroken lines)—it is solid or broken, depending on the value of your throw. When you have thrown the coins six times, you have created your hexagram. You then consult the table on page 202 to discover which hexagram you have created, and look that up in the list of 64 hexagrams on pages 203–207.

Always remember to create your hexagram from the bottom up.

Throwing the I Ching

All you need are three coins, each with its head and tail clearly marked, some paper and a pen. When drawing your hexagram, you always create it from the bottom up. This means that the first throw of the coins gives you the bottom (or sixth) line of the hexagram, and the final throw of the coins gives you the top (or first) line.

Decide which side of the coins is heads and which is tails. Throw the coins for the first time and count up their value, according to the guidelines below. As an example, let's say that your first throw is two heads (each with a value of two) and one tails (with a value of three). This adds up to seven (2 + 2 + 3), so you draw it as a solid line because it's an odd number. Throw the coins

again to create the next line of your hexagram, and continue until you have built up all six lines.

Heads = 2
Tails = 3
Even number = broken line
Odd number = solid line

To find your hexagram, look for your upper three lines along the top row of the table below, and your bottom three lines along the left-hand side of the table. The square where these columns meet gives the number of the hexagram.

Upper Trigrams

Lower Trigrams		Ch'ien	Chên	K'an	Kên	K'un	Sun	Li	Tui
	Ch'ien	1	34	5	26	11	9	14	43
	Chên	25	51	3	27	24	42	21	17
	K'an	6	40	29	4	7	59	64	47
	Kên	33	62	39	52	15	53	56	31
	K'un	12	16	8	23	2	20	35	45
	Sun	44	32	48	18	46	57	50	28
	Li	13	55	63	22	36	37	30	49
	Tui	10	54	60	41	19	61	38	58

The Hexagrams

Here are brief explanations of each of the 64 hexagrams, with their Chinese names. You can either use your intuition to expand their meaning or consult a more detailed I Ching reference book. Take time to consider how the message of the hexagram relates to your question.

1 Ch'ien All is going well. You are heading for success.

2 K'un For success, follow the path that has been set for you.

3 Chun Despite a bad start, your venture will be successful.

4 Mêng Someone needs your experience and your advice.

5 Hsü Take things slowly and gently. Wait for the right time to act.

6 Sung Compromise in an argument and don't be vengeful.

7 Shih Take control of the situation and control of yourself.

8 Pi Teamwork is better than solitary action.

9 Hsiao Ch'u Be patient, hold back and adopt a restrained approach.

10 Lü Behave with propriety and proceed with caution.

11 T'ai Difficulties are fading away. Your reputation is starting to grow.

12 P'i You're facing a stalemate because others are being petty.

13 T'ung Jên Be clear, honest and honorable in your relationships.

14 Ta Yu You will receive abundance on many levels.

15 Ch'ien It is better to be modest and humble than to be pompous.

16 Yü Enlist the help of others by enthusing them with your vision.

17 Sui Your conscience is your best guide as to how to behave.

18 Ku Wait three days before repairing the damage caused by previous mistakes.

19 Lin Adopting the correct approach will lead to joy and success.

20 Kuan Don't waste time on anything that's beyond your control.

21 Shih Ho You must overcome obstacles before you achieve success.

22 Pi Don't judge people or projects by their superficial appearance.

23 Po Something must come to an end before you start anything new.

24 Fu Situations are improving and you are back on a winning streak.

25 **Wu Wang** Act with honesty and integrity if you want success.

 26 **Ta Ch'u** Increase the number of people you know and work with.

 27 **I** Nourish others and yourself in every way, but do so with moderation.

 28 **Ta Kuo** A situation is becoming too stressful for you. Ask for help.

 29 **K'an** Life is hard, but you will survive if you're honest and keep your head.

 30 **Li** There is no point in fighting against the natural order of things.

31 **Hsien** You're attracted to someone, but must let nature take its course.

 32 **Hêng** The present situation is the best route to success and prosperity.

 33 **Tun** Retreating at the right time is your best tactic at the moment.

 34 **Ta Chuang** Don't confuse might with right. Behave honorably.

 35 **Chin** Act for other people's welfare as well as your own.

 36 **Ming I** Be modest and put your ambitions to one side at the moment.

 37 **Chia Jên** If you want success, don't try to be something you're not.

 38 **K'uei** Small steps will enable you to overcome your current problems.

39 Chien Retreat from a major obstacle and take a different course.

40 Hsieh Don't introduce new plans; focus on existing arrangements.

41 Sun Make conscious reductions in various areas of your life.

42 I Everything is going well and you will be successful. Be generous.

43 Kuai Focus on the truth, and be honest, earnest and sincere.

44 Kou Don't enter into partnerships with people you have only just met.

 45 Ts'ui Gather together with others and show them your respect.

 46 Shêng Success is on the way. You will pass a test with flying colors.

 47 K'un Accept the current situation and be optimistic about the future.

48 Ching There is more than enough to go round. Don't be greedy.

49 Kô This is a good time to introduce gradual changes to your life.

50 Ting Instigate change that will nourish everyone, including yourself.

51 Chên What seems like a shock will eventually lead to peace once more.

 52 Kên Stay in the here and now. Know when to act and when to rest.

53 Chien Do things in their correct order. Progress will be slow but steady.

 54 Kuei Mei Abandon a new project if it has too many pitfalls.

 55 Fêng Share your good fortune with others. Don't worry about losing it.

 56 Lü Humility, integrity and perseverance lead to success.

 57 Sun Focus on small improvements rather than major changes.

 58 Tui Behaving correctly and being firm will lead to joy and success.

59 Huan Success comes from being mindful of what you want to achieve.

 60 Chieh Limitations will give you a stable framework in which to operate.

 61 Chung Fu Follow what you believe and have faith in your convictions.

 62 Hsiao Kuo Aiming too high leads to possible peril and disappointment.

 63 Chi Chi Tidy up the loose ends in a project that's almost finished.

 **64 Wei Chi** Don't let complacency jeopardize a current project.

Runes

Runes have a special power and atmosphere, making them an intriguing psychic tool. They are said to have originated when Odin, the Norse god, suspended himself upside down from Yggdrasil, the Tree of the World, for nine days and nine nights without water or food in order to learn about life and death. At the end of this period he achieved enlightenment and saw the runes lying on the ground beneath him.

Runes are hundreds of years old, and as a result it can sometimes be difficult to grasp their meaning, because it isn't always presented in a very immediate form. Sometimes they speak symbolically, but once you are able to understand their messages, you will realize how powerful and accurate they are. You can either buy a set of runes or make your own by painting the symbols on to pebbles or something similar.

In addition to being a form of divination, runes are also an ancient alphabet. Translating your name into the runic alphabet gives you a sigil (a symbol with occult meaning), which is believed to confer power and good fortune on you.

Casting the runes can be as simple or as complicated as you wish to make it.

Right: Runes are made from a variety of materials, including wood, stone and plastic.

CASTING THE RUNES

This is very simple. If you wish, you can simply choose a rune whenever you need guidance, or you could select one at the start of each day. There are two popular methods of casting runes: you can either place them all face down on a flat surface and choose the ones that appeal to you, or you can draw them out of the bag in which you keep them.

WORKING WITH RUNES

It may take you a while to get used to the tone and mood of the runes, but once you do you will realize how helpful they are. The following interpretations of the runes are necessarily fairly basic, but your intuition will help you to expand on them. Invertible runes (which look different when reversed) have two meanings: when they're inverted, they have the opposite meaning to that of their upright position. Non-invertible runes look the same when reversed.

Drawing a single rune can give you valuable insight into what the coming day will bring.

The Elder Futhark

Although there is some discussion about the exact number of runes you should work with, most sets contain 24 runes, which are known as the Elder Futhark. Some sets contain an extra rune, which is blank and is known as "wyrd." This is only used when casting the runes and is said to represent a turning point in the life of the person who draws it.

The Elder Futhark is divided into three sections, or *aetts*, of eight runes, each of which is ruled by a particular god. The first aett is known as Freya's aett, and represents growth. The second is Haegl's aett, representing the elements. And the third is Tyr's aett, which represents courage.

The Runes

Fehu

This rune describes money, possessions, love and food. It speaks of the need to protect and appreciate whatever you value. When inverted, it warns of the loss of something valuable.

Thurisaz

You will experience a turbulent phase that is the catalyst for constructive change. Difficulties may erupt without warning. When inverted, the problems will be much less serious.

Uruz

Strength, courage and mental and physical stamina are required to face obstacles. You must take responsibility for your actions. When inverted, Uruz warns of being too aggressive.

Ansuz

This rune describes communication in all its forms, and contact with people you respect and admire. It speaks of the need to know yourself well. When inverted, there may be communication difficulties.

Raido

Journeys of all descriptions are covered by this rune, as well as the ability to rise above problems and put decisions into action. When inverted, a situation may be out of control.

Gebo

Gebo describes gifts, love and talents. You may be giving or receiving love, but you shouldn't expect it as your right. This rune also refers to working for a higher purpose. It's a non-invertible rune.

Kaunaz

You're burning with enthusiasm and energy, but you need to channel this in the right direction. Shed light on areas that have previously been dark. When inverted, Kaunaz describes ignorance and complacency.

Wunjo

This rune represents happiness, companionship and the ability to be content with what you have. It also tells you to be careful about what you wish for. When inverted, it means feeling cut off emotionally.

Hagalaz

You're facing a difficult situation, which is out of your hands. Learn from experience and trust that good will come from it. This is a non-invertible rune.

Isa

This rune describes situations that are in a state of limbo or which are frozen in some way, such as when you cling to the status quo and resist necessary change. This is a non-invertible rune.

Nauthiz

Nauthiz describes feeling needy. It tells you to sort out your priorities and face facts, in order to improve your situation. This is a non-invertible rune.

Jera

Jera describes the end of one cycle and the start of another, being in a state of transition or living in the past. It also warns against creating difficult karma for yourself. Jera is a non-invertible rune.

Eihwaz

This rune has links with the mysteries of life and death. It counsels you to show endurance when confronting problems, and to have the ability to keep on keeping on. Eihwaz is a non-invertible rune.

Algiz

This rune represents protection and the need for spiritual awareness. It can describe finding your spiritual path. When inverted, Algiz warns of being too defensive.

Perth

Look beyond the surface of life and gain greater self-knowledge. Pay attention to your dreams. Perth also describes birth in all its forms, literal and symbolic. When inverted, it speaks of unfounded fears.

Sowela

This is a very optimistic rune. It's telling you to keep going and to remain enthusiastic, even when times are hard. You will eventually achieve success. It is a non-invertible rune.

Teiwaz

Teiwaz describes bravery, competitiveness, strength of purpose, justice and victory. It often relates to battles that are fought for the common good. When inverted, it represents defeat.

Ehwaz

This rune describes all forms of travel, and the benefits of a fruitful partnership. It speaks of the need for cooperation and flexibility. When inverted, it means a betrayal of trust.

Berkana

Berkana depicts fertility in all its forms and is especially favorable for creative projects. It represents secrets that have yet to be uncovered. When inverted, it means an inability to grow.

Mannaz

You need to be considerate towards others, and to view difficult situations with objectivity and intelligence. When inverted, Mannaz means having a closed mind.

Laguz

Tune into your intuition and develop your psychic powers. Laguz can also describe a steady stream of something coming into your life. When inverted, it speaks of being overwhelmed by fear.

Othila

Othila symbolizes money, possessions, character traits and other inheritances that are passed from one generation to another. When inverted, it describes clinging to the past.

Inguz

Inguz describes the seed stage of projects and relationships, when they are beginning to develop. Inguz encourages you to appreciate life, even in adversity. Inguz is a non-invertible rune.

Dagaz

This rune is connected with fresh starts, whether these are mental, physical, emotional or spiritual. When life is difficult, Dagaz promises that it will improve. It is a non-invertible rune.

Other psychic tools

There are many other tools to boost your psychic ability, especially if you wish to practice divination. Ideally, you should experiment with them all until you find those that most appeal to you. For instance, you might discover that you're a skilled reader of tea leaves or you might develop a passion for ceromancy (see opposite page).

READING TEA LEAVES

This is a classic form of divination, and its beauty is that all you need is a pot of tea made with leaf tea, plus a cup and saucer. China tea is especially good for tea-leaf reading because its leaves vary in shape. Choose a cup with a round bowl and an undecorated interior. Pour out the tea and drink it while thinking of the question you wish to ask (this should not be a question that requires a Yes or No answer). When there is only a tiny amount of liquid left in the cup,

Take your time when looking for images in your tea cup. Here, a dog is clearly shown.

take the cup in your non-writing hand, close your eyes and ask your question. Turn the cup three times in a counterclockwise direction, then turn it upside down on its saucer and leave it to drain for about thirty seconds. Carefully turn the cup the right way up and interpret the patterns that the leaves have formed in the cup.

Leaves near the handle represent the person who has asked the question. Those on the left of the handle describe the past, and those on the right describe the present and the future. Leaves around the rim and upper third of the cup describe the immediate present and the next couple of days. Leaves in the middle third of the cup refer to the next two weeks, and those in the lower third of the cup and the base represent between two and four weeks away.

CEROMANCY

This ancient technique is the art of divining the future from melted wax. It is very simple and needs little equipment: a large candle (preferably colored so that the melted wax is easy

Choose a colored candle so you can easily see the shape of the melted wax.

to see in the water), a box of matches and a bowl of cold water. However, you must plan ahead, because the candle has to burn for at least an hour in order to accumulate a generous amount of wax. Make sure that the color of the candle forms a good contrast with the color of the bowl's interior, so that you can tell them apart.

When you're ready and the candle has produced plenty of liquid wax, carefully blow it out, then immediately ask your question (again this should not be a question that requires a Yes or No answer). Gently pour the wax into the bowl of water, keeping your mind on the question throughout. When the wax has set, you can begin to interpret its shape. Use your intuition and imagination for this. If you wish to take the wax shape out of the water to study it in greater detail, wait until it has set firmly to avoid either breaking it or spilling the still-molten wax.

DIVINATION THROUGH NATURE

As you begin to practice and develop your psychic abilities, you will find that you become much more receptive to your surroundings. Paying attention to the natural world and the messages it has for you will encourage the sense that you're at one with your surroundings and that there are no divisions between you.

Take note of your encounters with the animal and insect kingdoms. If you frequently attract butterflies, perhaps even to the extent of them alighting on your body for a few seconds, this may mean that you're going through a period of transition, in exactly the same way that a butterfly will emerge from its chrysalis, having completely changed its shape. Consider how this applies to your current situation.

Watch the clouds in the sky to see if they form meaningful shapes. Can you hear messages in birdsong? Ask a question when you're in your garden or in the countryside and wait to see what happens next. Is it answered in some way, perhaps by a bird immediately starting to sing? Be prepared to experiment and to trust your intuition.

Butterflies and moths have great symbolic meaning. They represent transformation.

Channeling
and spirit guides

What is channeling?

Channeling has become very popular during the past few years, although it has been practiced for many centuries. It is the art of receiving information from the spiritual, psychic or unseen realms and, in most cases, passing it on for the benefit of the rest of humanity. In other words, someone acts as a channel for the information. Some people do this purely for themselves, by channeling information that only applies to them. Others do it on a much broader basis. For instance, a healer might channel specific information about her patient's physical condition or treatment and pass this on to him, or someone might establish a firm link with a particular entity and publish the information that comes through in book form or as a CD.

IS IT THE SAME AS MEDIUMSHIP?

Mediumship is similar to channeling, in that the medium (or sensitive) is receiving information from the spirit realms. However, mediumship is usually directed at a particular person, and the medium gets in touch with this person's dead relatives or friends. Not everyone has the ability to be a medium, as it calls for very specific psychic abilities. Channeling, on the other hand, is available to anyone who wants to practice it, and often involves getting in touch with spirit entities who are not known to those who are either performing or witnessing the channeling. It therefore has a much more impersonal feel than mediumship, although that does not make it any less important or valuable.

Many people channel information without realizing it. Writers sometimes talk about the inspiration for a book coming out of nowhere, and that they feel the words were being dictated to them by a higher source. If you have ever surprised yourself by saying something immensely profound without any conscious effort, thought or knowledge, you may have been channeling that information.

You don't have to be a medium to be able to channel.

Famous examples of channeling

Many books have been channeled via spirit entities. They cover a wide range of styles, from the wordy and sometimes impenetrable to the chatty and easily accessible. There is something, it seems, for everyone. You may even have read some books without realizing that they were channeled, because sometimes there is no clue about their origins on the cover. Below are a few examples of celebrated spiritual teachers whose work is channeled. Others include Ramtha, who claims to be the spirit of a 35,000-year-old warrior from Atlantis and is channeled by J. Z. Knight; Emmanuel, who was channeled by Pat Rodegast; and Lazaris, a non-physical entity who channels through Jach Pursel.

WHITE EAGLE

Grace Cooke was a British medium who first connected with the spirit entity, White Eagle, as a child at the start of the 20th century. This close connection gradually evolved into a lifelong working partnership in which Grace Cooke channeled White Eagle's teachings, both in talks and books. White Eagle says he is the spokesman for a group known as the Star Brotherhood.

The White Eagle Lodge was founded in London in 1936, partly as a result of a series of messages from a spirit claiming to be Sir Arthur Conan Doyle. Other Lodges were founded around the world in the ensuing years.

SETH

Seth is the spirit entity who channeled his teachings through Jane Roberts for more than twenty years until her death in 1984. She worked while in a trance, and the first Seth book, *The Seth Material*, was published in 1970. Seth also wrote his own book, *Seth Speaks*, in which he dictated exactly what he wanted to say. He taught that we all create our own reality and are therefore entirely responsible for it.

Maurice Barbanell channeled the spirit of Silver Birch for 61 years.

holds workshops. Abraham teaches prosperity work.

A COURSE IN MIRACLES

This book was channeled by Dr. Helen Schucman, a research psychologist, and was first published in 1975. She was an atheist when she began the work and resented the Christian language of what she was channeling, but gradually became more accepting of it. There are claims—although not from Dr. Schucman—that the book was channeled from Jesus Christ. *A Course in Miracles* teaches how to tell the difference between our inner wisdom and our egos.

SILVER BIRCH

The non-physical entity known as Silver Birch claims to have lived over 3,000 years ago. Silver Birch's teachings were channeled by Maurice Barbanell, who was the founder and editor of *Psychic News* in Britain. Together, they produced several books about the existence of life after death.

ABRAHAM

Abraham is the name given to a group of spiritual teachers who are working through Esther Hicks. She has channeled several books and CDs, including *Ask and It Is Given*, and also

Learning to channel

The best way to learn to channel is with a trusted teacher. This person will be able to guide you through the entire process, teaching you how to take it gently and providing a safe space in which you can experiment. He will also know about the potential problems and setbacks of channeling, having experienced them himself while he was training. However, if it is not possible for you to find a teacher, you can train yourself to channel.

TEACHING YOURSELF

If you have decided to teach yourself, you must follow the preliminary stages very carefully. Don't be tempted to ignore them, or to dismiss them as boring and rush into the full channeling process immediately. Not only will you have confusing and frustrating results, but you might also attract negative entities that will want to trick you by masquerading as something they are not. This will be a waste of your time, at the very least. The preliminary stages include protecting yourself from any negative energies that might be attracted to you while you are working, and making sure that you are fully grounded in your body. At first you will probably feel self-conscious and anxious about whether anything is happening, so you also need to learn how to quieten your mind. Any form of meditation (see pages 232–235) will be good practice for this, because it helps train your mind to be still and to shake off the extraneous thoughts that wander through it.

FINDING TIME TO CHANNEL

Never choose a time for channeling when you might be interrupted. This can be dangerous, as the interruption will rudely jerk you out of your contemplative state and can have a harmful effect on your physical and

It's essential to protect yourself psychically before you begin each channeling session.

astral bodies. Even a ringing telephone can disturb you. Someone walking into the room and placing a hand on your shoulder can be even more disturbing, and might even make you ill for a short while.

CLEANSING YOUR ENERGY

The first step in preparing to channel is to cleanse yourself of all the energetic debris that has accumulated in your aura. Ideally you should also have a good sense of self-knowledge and should have dealt with many of your emotional hang-ups and difficulties. We all have these problems and some of them may never go away, but at least we can do our best to be aware of them; otherwise we are unconscious of many of our prejudices and emotional difficulties, and could easily project them on to others.

You have already learned how to cleanse your aura of energetic debris (see pages 92–95), so you must follow this procedure each time you want to channel. This is so that you will be in a calm state of mind, and won't attract any difficult energies that can feed on your jumbled emotions. For instance, if you start to channel while feeling angry, negative entities could be attracted to your emotional state and might use it to manipulate you or play games with you.

BEING GROUNDED AND BALANCED

When you have finished cleansing your energy, the next step is to ground and balance yourself. If you omit this step you will easily be thrown off-balance while channeling. You will also find it impossible to know whether what you are experiencing is coming from within yourself or from an outside source. It would be like already feeling dizzy and then stepping on to a boat in choppy waters: you wouldn't know whether the dizziness was caused by your own physical condition or by the turmoil in the water.

Follow the grounding exercises given earlier in the book (see pages 24–25). Although you might imagine that channeling would be so much more effective if you were ungrounded, in fact that is not true. Metaphorically speaking, you need to keep both feet on the ground, otherwise you will float

off like a kite in a high breeze. This will reduce or even eliminate your ability to distinguish between well-intentioned communications and mischievous ones.

PROTECTING YOURSELF

This step is essential if you are going to channel safely. Never, ever start a channeling session without protecting yourself properly from negative energies. One highly effective way to do this is to practice the exercise in which you surround yourself in a psychic bubble of light (see pages 104–105), and then take this one step further by mentally placing an equal-sided cross on the front and back of your solar-plexus chakra. You can place another cross above your crown chakra for extra protection.

After you've carried out this essential preparation, you can also protect yourself by ensuring that your intentions are pure, honest and loving.

Always keep both feet flat on the floor while you are channeling, so you stay grounded.

MEDITATION TO MEET YOUR GUIDE

The next step is to put yourself into a meditative state. We have already discussed different methods of meditation and their importance (see pages 44–45), not only as preparation for psychic work, but as helpful exercises in themselves. When preparing for channeling work, you need to create a meditation that will provide you with a safe inner place in which to receive the wisdom that you want to hear.

Here is a simple but powerful meditation, which will enable you to go deep within yourself and become receptive to the messages that you want to receive.

1 Having cleansed, grounded and protected yourself (see page 231), sit in a comfortable chair with both feet flat on the floor.

2 Close your eyes and breathe deeply in and out three times to relax. With each out-breath, feel any tension ebbing out of you. With each in-breath, feel peace and harmony entering your body.

3 Now imagine that you are standing in a favorite place in nature. It could be a special beach, a favorite stretch of countryside or a wonderful garden. Feel yourself standing there. Completely tune into your surroundings. Hear or see the birds singing, listen to the crash of the waves or the murmuring of the wind through the trees. Really *be* there.

4 When you are completely immersed in your surroundings, look around you. Notice a wide river close by and a bridge that crosses it. The river is too wide for you to see the other side without crossing the bridge. Begin to walk over the bridge, taking note of

what it looks and feels like. Listen to the sound of the river flowing beneath the bridge.

5 Cross to the other side of the river. At the bottom of the bridge is a gate. Open this gate and walk through it into beautiful, peaceful surroundings. Ahead of you is a large, lovely building. Notice every detail of what it looks like. Walk up to it and go through the main entrance. Inside, it feels safe and tranquil. Look around you. There is a door with your name written on it. Walk towards it and open it. Inside is a wise, kind guide who will be channeling his or her wisdom to you.

6 Greet your guide and enjoy your time together. Listen to what is said, and write it down, if this is appropriate and you receive the information in the form of words.

7 When you have finished talking to your guide, thank him or her and leave the room. Gently close the door behind you, then leave the building and retrace your steps to the gate at the bridge. Open the gate and step through it, making sure that you close it behind you. Hear or see it shut. Walk across the bridge until you reach the other side, then return to your starting point in the beautiful surroundings you chose.

8 Now begin to count backwards from five. With each number, you are gradually becoming more alert and aware of your surroundings. By the time you have counted down to one, you are completely awake and back in your chair.

9 Open your eyes, stretch your arms and legs, and wiggle your fingers and toes, so you are fully grounded again.

Checking the communication

If a man appeared on your doorstep out of the blue, saying he was from your bank and wanted to talk to you about your bank account, you would want some evidence that he was who he said he was, before you let him into your house. You need to be equally careful when making psychic connections with spirits. The fact that a spirit dwells on one of the astral planes is not an automatic testament to his honesty and good intentions. So when you make contact with a spirit you need to check that, just like the man from your bank, he is who and what he says he is.

Listen to your gut instincts, and especially to your physical reactions. For instance, take note if you start to feel anxious or ill when connecting with a spirit.

Be vigilant about checking that you've made contact with a well-intentioned spirit.

Quality control

• The first thing to check is how you feel when you have made contact with the spirit. Are you peaceful and calm? Do you feel safe and in good hands? Or are you uneasy and slightly apprehensive?

• This explains why it is so important to be grounded, calm and centered before beginning to channel: if you are already feeling agitated, you won't notice if such emotions begin to increase when you connect with a spirit.

• If you start to feel uneasy, worried or uncomfortable, you should end your connection with this spirit immediately. Such emotions are warning signs that something is wrong. Don't ignore them.

• The next step is to check the quality of what you're being told. No spirit worth listening to (and worth channeling) will ever be domineering, rude, aggressive, egotistical or manipulative.

• If you start to receive messages insisting that you do exactly what the spirit tells you, messages that are snide about people you know or blatantly egocentric, once again you should sever all communication with that spirit immediately.

• Finally, if you are still unsure or want further proof, you can ask the spirit three times if he comes from God. If he does, he will answer truthfully each time. If he doesn't, he will say so in his third answer.

Choosing your channeling

Channeling can take many forms, including receiving personal messages during meditation, channeling healing, automatic writing (see pages 176–179) and delivering channeled messages to other people.

To a large extent you will be unable to choose which forms of channeling to practice. Rather like wanting to play a musical instrument and then discovering which one suits you best, you will find that some forms of channeling flow better than others. For example, you might realize that something special happens each time you channel healing energy, and that this is the direction you should be taking. Alternatively, you might find it difficult to establish a channeled connection for healing, but have no problems when it comes to linking with a spirit guide to receive personal messages. So be prepared to experiment and to try a different technique if your first choice doesn't work out in the way you would like.

SELECTING YOUR TIME

Your daily schedule will determine the best times for you to channel. Obviously, if your mornings are a frantic rush to get the children washed, fed and off to school before you start your own work, they aren't the best times to channel. You need to be relaxed and calm, without having one eye permanently on the clock.

Another thing to consider is mealtimes. It isn't advisable to channel on a full stomach because this may make you sleepy or give you indigestion, so you should wait for a couple of hours after a meal before doing any channeling. You must also avoid channeling after drinking alcohol. It may feel as though the channeling is flowing brilliantly, but you won't be fully in control of what's happening and the alcohol in your system may attract unpleasant spirit entities. In time, if you are successful at channeling, you may even decide to give up all forms of alcohol because they mar the clarity of the communications you receive.

Set aside a time for channeling when you know you won't be disturbed or in a hurry.

Creating a ritual

When you are first learning to channel it can be very helpful to establish a preliminary ritual. This will put you in a peaceful, yet receptive, state of mind, so that the channels of communication will flow more easily. Even if your chosen ritual feels strange at first, it will soon become a comfortable habit. You will probably want to continue it, even if you become practiced in the art of channeling.

Lighting candles can help to put you in a restful mood, ready to start channeling.

A tealight in a container is a far safer option than an unattended candle.

You must also create a ritual that you can practice at the end of your sessions. It is essential that you treat channeling seriously and, as you become more accomplished at it, you will realize how sensitive you become to atmospheres and noise after you have finished your work. For instance, you will feel ill and disorientated if you finish channeling and then immediately go into a busy street or shop.

A STARTING RITUAL

There is no need to create a complicated set of rituals. You could simply light a white candle before you start work, provided that you make sure it will burn safely while you are channeling. Alternatively, you could burn a tealight in a saucer, which is a safer option. If you like the smell of incense, you could burn a stick of a special incense that you only use when channeling. You could also bless your room before starting to channel by making the sign of an equal-sided cross in each of the corners of the room.

AN ENDING RITUAL

When you have finished your channeling session, it is essential to stay quiet and peaceful for a while. Too much disturbance, noise or mental stimulation soon after channeling will make you feel ill. Sit in your chair until you feel ready to get up. Check that you are grounded and balanced (see pages 24–25) and protected (see pages 104–107), and blow out the candle or tealight if it is still burning.

Life after death

When you channel you will be making contact with spirit entities. Some of them might have been known to you personally, such as relatives or friends who have died. It is therefore important to have some understanding about what happens to us after we die.

If you believe in reincarnation, you will know that you have probably lived on this earth before. Therefore you have died before and, between incarnations,

Before channeling, make contact with your dead relatives by looking at their photos.

The different spirit realms

Many people believe in heaven, but it can mean different things to different people. There are numerous books describing heaven, often channeled from spirits who are there. One famous example is *Life in the World Unseen*, channeled by Anthony Borgia. The general consensus of opinion about these books is that there are many different levels in the afterlife and that we are sent to the one most suited to our spiritual development. For example, someone who was never very interested in spiritual or religious matters, or who was selfish or vindictive while on Earth, will be sent to a less elevated level than someone who spent her life developing her spirituality and leading a life of service to others. However, someone on a low spiritual plane is not being punished, and she always has the option of developing spiritually.

returned to whichever realm you came from. Yet, despite this, most of us have little or no memory of what happened to us when we died. Children often have a good recollection of where they have come from, but they're usually told that such knowledge is nothing more than fantasy and that they should stop telling tales. As a result, they start to forget.

MOVING ON

After someone dies, his spirit stays in realms that are accessible to the earth for some time. Often, the spirit will stay close to the earth because he is watching over loved ones who are still there and wants to be near them. Eventually his spirit will develop and move on to a higher plane.

Ghosts and poltergeists

Although you are unlikely ever to channel a ghost or poltergeist, it is important for you to understand what such things are. You may even be asked to help someone whose house contains a ghost or poltergeist. There are significant differences between these two forms of entities, which you need to understand in order to deal with them.

GHOSTS

You are much more likely to encounter a ghost than a poltergeist. Although old houses are usually considered to be the most likely haunt of ghosts, new houses can also attract spirits. So can roads, parks, gardens and anywhere else that is frequented by human beings.

When you believe that somewhere is haunted, you need to determine what sort of haunting it is. There are two types: a haunting by a ghost, who might behave in different ways at different times, and a repetitive haunting that is always the same, involving the same actions and sounds (see page 246).

When somewhere is haunted by a ghost, it's because a spirit entity has become attached to that place. This spirit doesn't realize it's dead, and has never been led towards the light so that it can move on to the spirit realms. The ghost continues to wander in the places that it knew in life, often feeling angry or puzzled that strangers have invaded what it believes is still its territory. The ghost has no sense of time and is not aware of the months or years that have elapsed since its physical death.

Sometimes the ghost doesn't realize it's dead because its death was so swift. This is particularly true in the areas around old battlefields, which are full of disembodied spirit entities. Occasionally the spirit refuses to move on because it has a materialistic attachment to the place where it lived. In all cases, the ghost needs to be

Visit a stately home or ancient building expressly to tune into the ghosts there.

Repetitive hauntings

The other type of haunting isn't caused by a ghost at all. It is a repetitive action that has somehow been impressed upon the atmosphere, in the same way that a video tape picks up images from a television. For instance, if a haunting always consists of the sound of feet climbing the stairs, and nothing else, that is a repetitive haunting. There are many examples of this type of haunting, and usually they are very dramatic. For instance, there is the ghost of a gray lady who is reputed to run across the grounds of Glamis Castle in Scotland, tearing compulsively at her mouth. This is all she ever does.

helped towards the light, where it can be received by angels and other entities who can help it progress and move away from the earth. However, this is skilled work and should not be practiced by people who don't know what they're doing.

POLTERGEISTS

Poltergeists are the stuff of horror films, although they don't only belong on celluloid. There are many recorded examples of poltergeist activity. The word "poltergeist" comes from the Germans and means "noisy ghost," which is a very accurate description. There is no mistaking poltergeist activity because it's so disruptive, noisy and disturbing. Often it involves objects moving around, apparently of their own volition. For instance, plates might hurl themselves against the wall, or windows might shatter of their own accord. In the vast majority of cases, the activity is mischievous and irritating rather than evil and malicious.

For many years paranormal researchers believed that poltergeist activity wasn't caused by a spirit, but instead was a physical externalization of the disturbed emotions of someone who lived in the house. Often this was thought to be a child or adolescent who was unconsciously triggering all the activity. However, some researchers now believe that this theory—while applicable in some cases—does not relate to all reported instances of poltergeist activity.

Glamis Castle is allegedly the most haunted stately home in Britain.

Types of guides

When you start to channel, you will want to make contact with a spirit guide. There are several categories of guides, and you may wish to choose a particular type with whom to make psychic contact.

SPIRIT GUIDES

We all have many spirit guides who watch over us. No one on earth is without their guides. Although you may not consciously be aware of them, you are accompanied throughout all your lives by a group of spirits who have watched over and guided you from your first incarnation on Earth, and who stay with you between each incarnation, when you return to the soul plane. They are with you while you undertake your review of your most recent life and all the actions that you took while on earth. It is their loving duty to be with you for many lifetimes, and they are always delighted when you start to become aware of them and wish to make contact.

GUARDIAN ANGEL

Spirit guides include your guardian angel, and you will discover how to invoke him or her later in this section (see pages 260–261). Guardian angels, in contrast to other forms of angel who have never incarnated, may have been human at one point. You may even have known them during some of your incarnations. For instance, a guardian angel may have incarnated as a beloved grandparent during one of your lifetimes in order to be close to you and guide you through some difficult experiences. After the grandparent has died, he or she once again adopts the role of your spiritual guardian angel.

CALLING ON OTHER GUIDES

In addition to your spirit guides, you can also call on other forms of guidance whenever you need specific help. In the rest of this section you will learn how to make contact with angels, archangels, gods and goddesses whenever you need their help.

Our guardian angel is with us from birth and supports us throughout our life.

Relatives and ancestors

Our relatives—especially parents, grandparents, aunts and uncles—care for us while they are alive and don't stop when their physical bodies die and their spirits pass on to the soul planes. They continue to take an interest in our lives, and in times of trouble will do their best to give us guidance in any way they can. These methods include appearing in our dreams, often to give us a message, and doing things that make us think of them, such as manifesting the smell of their favorite scent or cigar.

People who are just starting to learn about life after death, and the concept of the soul continuing to exist between lifetimes, are often rather worried by the thought that their relatives can keep an eye on them at any time of the day or night. They get the impression that their relatives are acting almost like voyeurs.

If someone loved you while she was alive, she'll continue to do so in spirit.

However, this is not what happens. Spirits on the soul planes need to lower their vibrations considerably in order to draw close to the earth and this takes a great deal of effort. They can't stay with us for long and nor are they meant to: they have their own work to do in whichever spirit realm they occupy.

Relatives who died long before you were born may be watching over you.

Grief

It is only human to grieve for someone when he dies. Although this is a natural response to a person's death, if someone continues to grieve for too long without making any progress, it can have a detrimental impact on the spirit for whom the grief is expressed. This sounds harsh, especially in cases where children have died before their parents, but such profound grief can hold the spirit back and keep him tethered to Earth. It is also extremely upsetting for the spirit, who can't comfort the grieving person and explain that he is healthy, happy and no longer in any distress.

Contacting relatives

It is very reassuring to make contact occasionally with a treasured relative who is now in the spirit world. Many people take great comfort from knowing that their parents or grandparents are still keeping an eye on them, even though they left their physical bodies many years ago. They are aware of the tremendous amount of love that is being sent to them from the soul planes, especially when they're going through difficult experiences.

We all need help and support when times are hard or we don't know which action to take for the best. We might ask our friends for advice, so it is only natural to ask our relatives as well, whether they are still on Earth or have moved on to the spirit realms. However, although we like to listen to the advice we receive and be given guidance, there always comes a time when we have to stand on our own two feet and take responsibility for our own actions. Just as our friends would soon get fed up with us if we pestered them day and

night for advice on everything from what to eat for lunch to which clothes to wear each morning, so the spirit world can get tired of being bombarded with questions from those who are seemingly incapable of making a decision about anything. So, if you wish to make contact with a relative or ancestor in the spirit realms—especially when you're seeking answers to questions about the direction your life is taking—don't expect to be told exactly what to do or to tune in on a daily basis for your latest batch of advice. It doesn't work like that!

MAKING CONTACT

When you want to contact a dead relative or ancestor, you need to prepare yourself in exactly the same way as for any other sort of channeling (see pages 228–231). The fact that you may have known this person very well for a long time, and that you love each other, doesn't counteract the need to protect yourself from unseen entities and from

Consider contacting someone you loved very much, such as a favorite aunt.

the physical shock to your body if there are sudden interruptions in the middle of channeling.

Also, just as in any other form of channeling, you must test the quality of the communication to check that it is indeed from the person you wish to contact (see pages 236–237). However, the quality and purity of your intention will help to protect you. If you're making contact because of genuine love for the person in the spirit world, this will give you much more protection

than if you're getting in touch because you want to ask your uncle where he hid all his money or whether he'll tell you the winner of the next big horse race. Such motives are more likely to attract unpleasant entities that will feed on your emotions.

ESTABLISHING A CONNECTION

Follow the preparation guidelines for other forms of channeling. Ideally you should think about making contact with your relative or ancestor in advance, to give him time to rearrange his own schedule if necessary so that he'll be available. Contrary to popular opinion, spirits don't spend their time sitting on fluffy clouds playing harps.

It will help to sit with a photograph or portrait of the person you wish to contact. Alternatively, you could sit holding one of his personal belongings, such as his watch. Focus your thoughts on the person and let a sense of pure love flow through you, filling your heart chakra (see pages 72–73) with a warm glow. You are now ready to begin the meditation that will bring you into contact with your relative or ancestor.

MEDITATION TO CONTACT A RELATIVE

1 Cleanse, ground and balance yourself (see pages 24-25) and protect yourself (see pages 104–107) in the usual way, then sit in a comfortable chair with both feet flat on the floor.

2 Close your eyes and breathe deeply in and out three times to relax. With each out-breath, feel any tension ebbing out of you. With each in-breath, feel peace and harmony entering your body.

3 Now imagine that you're standing in a favorite place in nature. It could be a special beach, a favorite stretch of countryside or a wonderful garden. Feel yourself standing there. Completely tune into your surroundings. Hear or see the birds singing, listen to the crash of the waves or the murmuring of the wind through the trees. Really *be* there.

4 When you are completely immersed in your surroundings, look around you. Notice that there is a wide river close by, and that a bridge crosses it. The river is too wide for you to see the other side without crossing the bridge. Begin to walk over it, taking note of what it looks and feels like. Listen to the sound of the river flowing beneath the bridge.

5 Cross the bridge to the other side of the river. At the bottom of the bridge is a gate. Open this gate and walk through it (closing it behind you) into beautiful, peaceful surroundings. Ahead of you is the house where your relative or ancestor lived. If you don't know what this house looked like, trust the image that comes to you. See the house in all its many details. Notice the roof and the chimney. Look at the windows and the doors. Walk towards the house and enter the garden that lies in front of the house. Look at the plants in the garden.

6 There is a large, old apple tree in the front garden. Your relative is sitting in a chair underneath it. There is another chair, for you. It looks comfortable and inviting. Greet your relative warmly, as you would have done in life, and thank him for meeting you. If you never met while the relative or ancestor was alive, politely introduce yourself and explain why you have asked for this meeting.

7 Sit down and begin your conversation with your relative. Listen to what is said, and write it down, if this is appropriate and you receive the information in the form of words.

8 When your conversation is over, thank your relative and say good-bye to him. Walk out of the garden towards the bridge and the gate at the foot of the bridge. Open the gate and step through it, making sure that you close it behind you. Hear or see it shut. Walk across the bridge until you reach the other side, then return to your starting point in the beautiful surroundings you chose.

9 Now begin to count backwards from five. With each number, you are gradually becoming more alert and aware of your surroundings. By the time you have counted down to one, you are completely awake and back in your chair.

10 Open your eyes, stretch your arms and legs, and wiggle your fingers and toes.

Angels

Angelic help is all around us. All we have to do is ask for it. There are times when we receive angelic help without requesting it first, although we may not realize that is what's happening. There are many documented cases of angelic intervention, usually in dramatic circumstances. For example, you might trip over in the middle of a busy road and be helped to your feet—just before a bus bears down on you—by a man who seems to have appeared out of nowhere. The man gently steers you to safety and you thank him, but then when you look around for him, he has vanished. He may have been an angel, sent to save you from being run over by the bus.

Angels can also appear in less threatening circumstances. Have you ever had an impromptu chat with a passing stranger that felt as though it went beyond the boundaries of normal, everyday conversation? Perhaps this person said something to you that set you thinking, guided you in a new direction or answered a question you'd been wrestling with for a long time. That person may have been an angel sent to help you.

Angels are waiting to be summoned. Get into the habit of working with them every day.

There is an angel looking after each country throughout the world.

REQUESTING HELP

These are examples of angels who appear exactly when we need them, without us consciously summoning them. But at other times it is very helpful to ask for an angel to help you for a specific purpose. You might like to ask your guardian angel to do this, or you may prefer to contact an angel who specializes in your particular need. In the rest of this section you will find descriptions of angels that you can summon, as well as information about the areas in which they love to help, and ways to invoke them. And you will also find information on how to invoke your own guardian angel, as well as the angel who looks after your home.

Your guardian angel

Everyone has a guardian angel. You have one, even if you aren't yet aware of his (or her) presence. This angel is with you throughout your life, standing closer to you than you could ever believe. Your guardian angel is with you through your triumphs and tragedies, as well as during those nondescript days when your life simply jogs along. When you die, your guardian angel is still with you, helping you to make your transition into the spirit life. And this angel will repeat the entire process when you are next incarnated on earth.

What many people find so difficult to understand is that they have to ask their guardian angel for help before he can intercede on their behalf. He has to obey the spiritual law that says help can only be given when it's asked for; otherwise, it's an act of interference. Your guardian angel longs to be asked to help, because then he can truly be of service to you. However, he has to be asked each time you need his assistance. It isn't enough for you to ask him for

Your guardian angel can only come to your aid when you ask for help.

help once and then imagine that he'll spring into action whenever you need him. You must ask him every time.

SUMMONING YOUR ANGEL

1 To invoke your guardian angel, find a quiet time when you won't be disturbed.

2 You can either speak to him aloud or in your head, although your invocation is much stronger when spoken, and you should speak from your heart. For instance, you could say, "Dear guardian angel, thank you for being with me at this moment. Please help me to [describe the help you want], so that the outcome is for the highest good of everyone concerned."

3 It is polite to thank your angel when he's given you his help, even if you haven't yet received the benefits. Simply know that these will come, and show your gratitude for them.

The hierarchy of angels

Angels are believed to be benevolent messengers from God. Traditional belief states that they are pure spirits who have never incarnated as human beings, although some writers dispute this. Angels frequently play a starring role in both the Old and New Testaments in the Bible, although their role is not confined to Christianity. For example, it was the Archangel Gabriel who brought the news to Mary that she was going to give birth to the son of God, and it was this same angel who, as the Spirit of Truth, dictated the Koran to Mohammed. In the 15th century Joan of Arc claimed that it was Gabriel who told her to rescue France from the invading English army.

THE ANGELIC REALMS

Although there are many ancient and diverse writings on the subject of angels, a few theories have become accepted and are still in use today. One of these was postulated by Dionysius the Areopagite, a Greek mystic, in the 6th century CE. He wrote the *Celestial Hierarchy*, in which he divided the angelic realm into nine orders, consisting of three choirs. St. Thomas Aquinas, the 13th-century Italian theologian, later developed this theory, while honoring the structure of Dionysius' hierarchies.

THE FIRST CHOIR

These three orders of angels are nearest to God and, according to St. Thomas Aquinas, are dedicated to face-to-face worship of God.

Seraphim

These are closest of all the angelic orders to God and, as a result, are often known as the "burning ones" because they are aflame with love and devotion to God. They include Uriel and Michael.

Cherubim

These form the next order of angels. Their name means "one who intercedes," and they have a protective role that was first assigned to them in ancient Assyria, when they were depicted as having large, winged animal bodies and human faces. God positioned them in the east of the Garden of Eden, and later their image was engraved on the Ark of the Covenant. They include Jophiel and Gabriel.

Thrones

Also known as "the many-eyed ones," these angels are depicted as wheels of Divine fire that surround God's throne. They carry out God's decisions and are the angels of justice. They include Japhkiel and Raziel.

Left: Uriel is associated with light.

Raziel, one of the Thrones, has knowledge of all the secrets of the universe.

THE SECOND CHOIR

According to the writings of St. Thomas Aquinas, this second order of angels is dedicated to knowledge of God through the universe.

Dominions

God shows his mercy through the angels in the Dominions, who bring wisdom and knowledge. They each carry a scepter and sword, showing God's power throughout all creation. They include Zadkiel and Zacharel.

Zadkiel belongs to the Dominions. He's the angel of mercy and compassion.

Virtues

These are the angels who show courage, earning them the name "the shining ones." They work in conjunction with the Thrones (members of the first choir) to bring blessings and rewards to human beings who have mastered their difficulties. They include Haniel.

Powers

These angels work fearlessly and tirelessly to keep fallen angels and so-called devils from taking over the universe. The Powers include the Angels of Death and Birth. When we die, the Powers guide us through our transition into the next phase of our lives. They are believed to be led by Chamuel.

THE THIRD CHOIR

These are the angels who are dedicated to taking care of human beings, and are therefore known as ministering angels.

Principalities

These angels guard the world's nations, as well as their leaders. They also guard the world's religions, as well as countries, big organizations and sacred places. They are said to include Raguel.

Archangels

These are the chief angels, carrying God's messages to humans. Each of them has a masculine and feminine aspect. Each one is also connected to a particular element, whether that is fire, earth, air or water. They have control over the many armies of angels who continually battle against the forces of darkness. There is some debate over how many Archangels there are, but they are generally considered to include Michael, Gabriel and Raphael.

Angels

Although these angels are assigned the lowest rank in the hierarchy, that doesn't mean they are less important than the rest of their angelic brethren. Angels work as everyday intermediaries between God and humans, and between God and nature. They include each human's guardian angels. All these angels are waiting to be summoned by us whenever we need them.

Chamuel is the angel of love. He also specializes in helping us to find lost objects.

Invoking angels

If you want an angel to help you, you must consciously ask for assistance. But how do you do this? Should you only ask for help when you are in a quiet place, in a meditative state or when you believe that you have been virtuous? Will an angel still come to your aid if you have behaved badly or if you're in the middle of somewhere hectic, such as a busy department store on Christmas Eve?

Angels often leave a white feather as their calling card.

There is no need to worry. Angels come to our assistance whenever and wherever we summon them. They are happy to help us, although it is only good manners on our part to ask politely for their help and to thank them for coming to our aid.

WHAT TO ASK FOR

You may feel that your request for angelic assistance isn't really special enough to deserve a response. For example, if you will be taking a long journey and you're worried about missing your plane or encountering traffic jams on the roads, you might think these concerns are too trivial for you to bother the angelic realms with them.

Actually there is no cut-off point at which angels won't help you because it is not worth their time. They will always help, even if you consider your request to be extremely minor. Many people regularly ask angels for help in

Signs of angelic help

How simple and gratifying it would be if, every time you asked for angelic help, you received it loud and clear, with no confusion or hesitation. However, that isn't necessarily what happens. Instead of having an angel materialize in front of you, complete with wings and halo, who does whatever you want and then disappears again, you will probably have to rely on more subtle clues that you have received angelic help.

For instance, you might have a sudden flash of inspiration; someone may offer you precisely the information you have been looking for; or the seemingly intractable problem that has dragged on for months might magically sort itself out. Alternatively, you may suddenly feel overwhelmed by a sense of love and well-being. Another sign that an angel has been near is when you find a white feather in a place where you weren't expecting it.

finding parking places, for instance. The very fact that you need help with something means they will gladly come to your aid. However, angels won't help if your request involves bringing harm to another person, such as wanting to exact revenge. In fact, the energy will rebound on you, with unpleasant consequences.

HOW TO ASK FOR HELP

You can ask for help anywhere, at any time. You don't have to be in a special or sacred place. Simply request assistance, either silently or out loud, and trust that it will arrive. Always remember to ask politely, and to thank the angel for arriving, because this will help to attune you energetically to the angel's presence.

INVOKING THE ANGEL OF YOUR HOME

If you want to begin to work with angels, one of the best ways to start is with your own home. Each home has its own angel, although most of us aren't aware of this. If you want to create a more peaceful and tranquil atmosphere around you, or you simply want to invite as much angelic input into your life as possible, you can invoke your own home's angel on a daily basis.

1 Select an area of a room that you can dedicate to the angel, such as the mantelpiece in your sitting room or a corner of the chest of drawers in your bedroom. Make sure it is clean and tidy, then decorate it with a vase of fresh flowers, a candle, a crystal, a beautiful shell, a picture of an angel or anything else that you feel is appropriate. This will be your altar.

2 Each morning, shortly after you have woken up, when you're feeling calm and relaxed, stand in front of your altar and greet the angel of your home. You can either do this out loud or in your head. Thank the angel for being with you, and pay attention to your feelings and impressions. Sometimes you will know when the angel has drawn near because the mood in the room will lighten or the air will become thicker. You might even smell flowers or hear strains of music. Even if you don't sense anything, know that the angel of your home is with you.

3 If you have a request, voice it politely and considerately, asking for the highest good for everyone concerned, then once again thank the angel for helping you.

INVOKING ANGELS FOR SPECIFIC PURPOSES

Each angel has its own allotted tasks to carry out in the universe, and these include helping human beings as we go about our everyday lives. There are countless angels, each of whom has a specific role to play, and it is beyond the scope of this book to list them all. However, here are a few angels whom you might like to invoke, according to your need. If you're worried about remembering which angel fulfills which purpose, or if the angel you need isn't listed here, simply ask for the right angel to be sent to you and know that this will happen.

Here on Earth, we deal in linear time and, as we often say to each other when feeling harassed, we can't be in two places at once. Happily, angels have no such restrictions. They can be in many different places at the same time, so there is no need to worry that if you invoke Archangel Michael you will be put on his waiting list and have to wait weeks for him to arrive because he has lots of other people to help first. He will be with you instantly.

Archangel Gabriel

Gabriel means "God is my strength." Unlike all the other angels in the upper angelic strata, Gabriel is generally believed to be female. Her chief role is as God's messenger, sending important communications to human beings. Therefore she is the angel to invoke if you want to improve the way you communicate with the rest of the world, wish to receive Divine inspiration while

Gabriel enables us to connect with our Divine potential and to realize it.

Michael is the angel of courage.

working on a creative or artistic project, or want God to guide you in reaching a decision. Gabriel is also the angel to call on when you want guidance about conceiving or giving birth to a child.

Archangel Michael

Michael, whose name means "look like God," is usually depicted holding a sword and the scales of justice with which he slays the dragon or fights Satan. It is his role to combat the negativity and fear in the world. Therefore he is the angel to invoke when you need courage and determination, or when you have become bogged down in pessimistic and gloomy thoughts. He will also give you guidance if you are unsure about which direction to take in life.

Archangel Uriel

Uriel is the Regent of the Sun and his symbol is an open hand holding a flame. His name means "fire of God" and he is the most radiant of all the angels. He is the angel of "thunder and terror," and is therefore the one to invoke if you need help with the weather, and especially if you're concerned about impending serious weather or if you're coping with its aftermath. Uriel is also the angel to call on if you want help in achieving your full potential and in gaining increased understanding of who you are.

Archangel Metatron

Metatron is a special angel because he was once human. It is believed that he was originally the prophet Enoch, who

Metatron is a good angel to invoke if you're trying to motivate yourself into action.

was a scribe, and that God sent him up to the seventh heaven (the highest realm of heaven), where he continues his work by keeping the Akashic Records, also known as The Book of Life. Therefore Metatron is the angel to invoke when you need help with writing. He will also help you to achieve your potential as a loving and considerate human being. The meaning of his name is uncertain.

Archangel Raphael

Raphael means "God has healed," and he is often pictured holding a caduceus, or a staff around which two snakes are entwined. The caduceus is the classic symbol of healing, and so Raphael is the angel to call on when you want to receive Divine healing or send it to someone else.

Raphael also sends healing to animals, so he is the angel to contact if you're worried about your pet's health. Healers can work with Raphael, asking him for guidance. Perhaps because of his healing work, he is believed to be the most friendly and approachable of all the angels.

Archangel Raguel

His name means "friend of God," and Raguel's task is to create harmony and order among his fellow archangels and angels. He is equally skilled at bringing harmony to problematic human relationships, and is the angel to invoke when you're caught up in conflict with someone. He helps to resolve arguments and disputes of all kinds, and is also good at championing the cause of the underdog.

Archangel Haniel

In ancient Babylonian times Haniel worked as a Divine emissary to the priest-astronomers who were studying astrology and other forms of divination. He also helped them to understand the power and energy of the moon, and to connect with their spiritual power. Haniel is therefore the angel to call on when you want help and guidance in strengthening your psychic abilities or in working closely with lunar energy. Haniel means "grace of God," and we can ask him to bring more grace into our lives, especially in the form of loving friends and family.

Haniel works to bring us a greater sense of grace and emotional fulfillment.

Above: Raphael is the angel to call on if you want help with any form of healing.

Master spirits

In addition to contacting angels for help, you can also make contact with master spirits. These are the great teachers or prophets, also known as ascended masters, who once lived on Earth and who have long been recognized and revered for their pure spirituality and wisdom. They come from every religion, culture and civilization, although you don't have to practice the faith with which they are associated in order to make psychic contact with them. Gods and goddesses are another branch of master spirits with whom you can connect. If you always thought they belonged only in the pages of books about myths, you could be in for a big surprise!

DARING TO MAKE CONTACT
If you are new to the concept of contacting a master spirit, the idea can seem rather strange and possibly even

You don't have to be a practicing Buddhist to gain peace from a statue of Buddha.

You may decide to work exclusively with one master spirit, such as Buddha or Ganesha.

Examples of master spirits

There are many ascended masters, all of whom live in the spirit world and have vowed to dedicate themselves to helping humans learn and progress through their many incarnations on Earth. These master souls have all delayed their own progress through the higher realms of heaven in order to stay close to us and help us. They include Jesus Christ, the Virgin Mary, Buddha, Kuan Yin, Maitreya, Krishna and Babaji (see pages 278–279).

Many gods and goddesses are also waiting to come to our aid. Like ascended masters, they come from every culture, including Greek, Indian, Egyptian, Irish and British. They include Ganesha, Vesta, Athene, Lakshmi, Thoth and Brigit (see pages 280–281).

slightly daunting. This is especially true if you were raised in a Western orthodox religion, which taught that the only route to its particular ascended master was through its church. You may doubt that you will be able to make contact with your chosen master spirit yourself, without a priest or minister acting as an intermediary. You might even have been taught that direct contact is blasphemous or forbidden. Or you may simply feel that you are not "good" enough to make contact yourself. It can be difficult to get past these ingrained rules.

However, as far as the master spirits are concerned, none of this matters. They have dedicated themselves to helping humans and that is what they want to do. If a human needs their help, they are delighted to give it. As with angels, the importance of your request is immaterial. Master spirits don't have a scale against which they measure the seriousness of your need; they simply hear your request and hurry to meet it.

GO IN PEACE

When asking a master spirit for help, you must make sure your request doesn't involve deliberately harming another person. Your intention is very important, so you must get it right. Ideally, each time you should ask that the outcome of your request is for the highest good of all concerned. This will show that your intentions are pure and you have everyone's best intentions at heart.

MAKING YOUR REQUEST

How should you approach a master spirit? You may feel relaxed about talking to an angel, but become much more self-conscious when you want to speak directly to Jesus or Buddha. Should you kneel, say a prayer first, or light a candle? You can do any or all of these things if it feels right, and if you wish you can meditate first so that you're in a calm and contemplative frame of mind. Alternatively, you could contact one of the master spirits during your meditation. However, life is not always that simple, and there could well be times when you need to make contact in less auspicious or peaceful surroundings. Therefore you may prefer to train yourself to initiate contact with a master spirit during your day-to-day activities. He or she will not mind.

Invoking the master spirits

When you feel ready to invoke a master spirit, all you need to do is think of the one you wish to contact and make your request. As with angels, each master spirit performs a different duty towards the human and animal races. Therefore

After becoming enlightened, Kuan Yin chose to stay in human form to help all beings.

you may wish to choose the master spirit who is most in tune with the nature of your request, having referred to the list below. Alternatively, you can simply ask that your request is granted by whichever master spirit is most suited to the task.

When you feel a master spirit draw near, politely ask his or her name. If you doubt the authenticity of the spirit who has contacted you (occasionally you may connect with a mischievous spirit who is pretending to be something it is not), ask it three times if its intentions are pure. It is spiritual law that the third answer must contain the truth.

AREAS OF SPECIALIZATION

This list gives a brief rundown of the areas that particular master spirits specialize in, which may be useful when deciding which one to invoke.

Jesus Christ

As he was in life, Jesus is a miraculous healer. Call on him when you want help in either healing yourself or someone else. Hand over your problems into his care. His presence always brings a deep sense of peace and love.

The Virgin Mary

The mother of Jesus has a sweet, loving presence. She is the protector of all children, so you can invoke her whenever you need help with a child. Her mercy is boundless.

Buddha

Buddha teaches us the importance of moderation, and that desires lead to suffering. If we can release these desires, we are freed from all suffering. When you invoke him, he brings balance, peace and a strong sense of calm.

Kuan Yin

The Buddhist goddess of compassion, Kuan Yin helps us to show increased compassion both to ourselves and others. Her name means "hear world sounds," and she promises that she will come to the aid of anyone who calls.

Maitreya

He is often known as the Buddha of the Future, who will succeed Shakyamuni Buddha. His name means "loving kindness," and he is often represented as the Laughing Buddha who brings joy and laughter.

Krishna is the god to invoke if you want to bless your food and drink.

Babaji

Babaji was a man, often called the Yogi-Christ, who lived in the Himalayas from 1970 to 1984. He is known as "the deathless avatar," because he is thought to have been in a physical form for centuries. Babaji is also believed to be the latest incarnation of the Divine. You only have to speak his name with reverence to receive his blessing.

Ganesha

With his sweet nature, Ganesha is one of the most beloved Hindu gods. He is the god to invoke when you want to start a new venture, because he will give it his blessing. He will also help you to overcome obstacles.

Vesta

This is the Roman name for the goddess of the hearth, who was known to the Greeks as Hestia. Ask for her help when you are concerned about your home or family, or when you're looking for the perfect home in which to live.

Krishna

One of the three great Hindu gods, Krishna is a Divine hero who brings blessings, joy and love. He is connected with food, so you can invoke him to bless the food you eat (see pages 116–119).

Athene

She is the Greek goddess of wisdom and her symbol is an owl. Invoke her whenever you need help in reaching decisions or in gaining a clear, objective view of a situation that is troubling you.

Lakshmi

She is the Hindu goddess who was married to Vishnu in each of their incarnations. Considered the epitome of wifely perfection, she is the goddess to invoke when you need help in healing a relationship. You can also ask her to bring abundance into your life and to increase your sense of fulfillment.

Thoth

Thoth is the Egyptian god of secret knowledge and writing. Invoke him when you need help in putting your thoughts into words, and when studying occult subjects.

Brigit

There are several variations on the spelling of this Celtic goddess's name. Ask for her help when you want to conceive a child or need her protection during childbirth.

If you call on her, Brigit will help you when you're concerned about your children.

Psychic love
and soulmates

What is a soulmate?

If you have ever met someone and felt an immediate affinity with her, such as affection, familiarity or even love, that person may be a soulmate. Equally, if you have ever met someone and experienced an instinctive fear or dislike of him, he might also be a soulmate. Both these relationships come under the category of psychic love, which describes any type of relationship in which there is a lesson to be learned, a past-life connection or a strong psychic link. In fact it may be that every relationship, however fleeting, is some form of psychic love, because they each have something to teach us.

A soulmate is someone you have known in a previous life, and often in many past lives. During your numerous incarnations your relationship with this person will have gone through a wide variety of expressions, such as that of brother and sister, husband and wife, parent and child, teacher and pupil, boss and employee or doctor and patient. You may also have experienced troubled

relationships with one another, such as persecutor and persecuted, or victim and aggressor. You may even be experiencing a difficult relationship in your present incarnation.

SAME SOULS, DIFFERENT RELATIONSHIPS

We don't always perform the same role with each other, because we need to explore the connection that we share in all its different facets. For instance, two souls wouldn't learn the many lessons they needed if they always reincarnated as a husband and wife who enjoyed a blissful marriage. Sometimes we need to work out the karma (which, put very simply, means the debts and rewards) that has built up between us during our shared incarnations, and this is not always a comfortable experience. For example, if two soulmates were lovers in a previous life, but their relationship ended because one of them was unfaithful, the roles might be reversed in their next shared incarnation.

Your relationship with a soulmate may be a romantic one but this doesn't always apply.

AGREEING TO DIFFER

Soulmates agree on the script of their next relationship while they are on the soul plane between lives. They discuss what they need to learn from each other and plan how this can be enacted. They might agree to enjoy a wildly romantic love affair that lasts for only a short time, or they could be best friends who meet at school and are only parted in old age by death. Alternatively, regardless of the love their souls share, they could decide that their next relationship will be fraught with problems and animosity. You could look on this as a form of role-play, perhaps with one soul playing the "good guy" and the other the "bad guy." We will discuss this sort of relationship in more detail later in this section.

Someone who is your sister in one lifetime may be your boss next time around.

Soul groups

We don't have just one soulmate. We all have many of them, and they usually reincarnate at roughly the same time as us, so that we will share at least part of our lifetimes with each other. These people belong to what is called our "soul group," meaning a group of souls who stay together through many lives. In each incarnation we play a different role for each other. You could think of it as being like a repertory company, in which the same souls play different roles in each lifetime.

We don't always have an intense relationship on earth with each member of our soul group. We might know some of the members of our soul group only briefly in a particular lifetime. For instance, the colleague you loved working with for six months and then never saw again might be a member of your soul group who fleetingly entered your life before disappearing. The unpleasant neighbor, who makes your heart sink every time you catch sight of her, may also be a member of your soul group. Perhaps she has agreed to teach you a lesson about fortitude or compassion, and you have agreed to teach her a lesson about unconditional love.

The members of your immediate family, and your close friends, are likely to belong to your soul group. Other people who touch your life, but with whom you aren't so closely involved, may also be members of that group.

Twin flames

The notion of twin flames was famously mentioned by Plato in his *Symposium*. He suggested that each human was originally two people contained within one body, with two heads, four arms and four legs. They were very happy in this state—so happy, in fact, that they became ultra-confident and challenged the gods. Zeus, furious at this, retaliated by splitting each human in two, so the two halves were separated and spent the rest of their lifetimes searching for each other.

Twin flames are believed to be different from soulmates, because they come from the same person. Your twin flame is truly your other half, and when you find him or her you will feel complete. However, twin flames are notoriously elusive, and often your twin flame will be on the soul planes while you are on Earth, and vice versa. It is thought by some authorities that when two twin flames are finally reunited on Earth, they will experience their last earthly incarnation.

FINDING "THE ONE"

The idea of finding your twin flame is very seductive, and for some people it means that they reject every relationship in turn because it is not "the one." They can tell that they haven't yet found their twin flame, because there aren't enough similarities between them. As in the case of many identical twins who are separated at birth, when twin flames discover each other, they find that their lives have run almost parallel. They have the same likes and dislikes, the same experiences, they may even have lived in the same places or share a love for the same countries.

Interestingly, it has been discovered that more than fifty percent of pregnancies begin as twin pregnancies. In the majority of cases one of the fetuses dies, whether it is absorbed into the body of the other twin while in the womb or is stillborn. Perhaps these are examples where the twin flames are together in the womb for a short while before they separate again?

*A relationship with a twin flame is intense and
truly feels like meeting your other half.*

Reincarnation

In order to believe in soulmates who have shared many lifetimes, you have to believe in reincarnation. This is the concept that a soul dies and is reborn on Earth many times. During each lifetime the soul develops and tries to work out the karma that has accrued from previous lives.

RELIGIOUS ATTITUDE

Reincarnation is a belief that spans many of the world's great religions. Hinduism, Jainism, Sikhism, Tibetan Buddhism and the Kabbalah all teach the importance of reincarnation. It was once part of Christianity, too, until virtually all mention of reincarnation and karma was edited out of the Bible at the Second Council of Constantinople in 553 CE. However, the Gnostic gospels, which were discovered in 1945 and are thought to have been

A child prodigy may be expressing a talent that she had in her previous life.

written about one hundred years after Christ's birth, speak quite clearly of reincarnation and karma.

REINCARNATION IN TIBET

There are some well-known cases that point to the existence of reincarnation. The most famous is probably that of the lineage of the Dalai Lamas: each one is believed to be the reincarnation of the previous Dalai Lama. The 14th Dalai Lama was found when he was a small boy called Lhamo Dhondrub in a remote village in Tibet. He recognized Lama Kewtsang Rinpoche, who came to see him in disguise, spoke to him in the Lhasa dialect that he would have used in his previous incarnation and also recognized the lama's servant, Amdo Kasang, who was pretending to be the leader of the party. He then correctly identified various possessions that had belonged to Thupten Gyatso, the 13th Dalai Lama. His body also bore specific marks that are associated with each Dalai Lama. Finally, he described the box in which the 13th Dalai Lama's false teeth were stored. By this point, there was no mistaking the fact that the small boy was indeed the reincarnation of the 13th Dalai Lama.

CULTURAL ATTITUDES

Some cultures are much more receptive to the idea of reincarnation than others. There are many documented cases in India, especially those involving small children who insist that they aren't living with their "real" families and belong elsewhere, such as in another town with another family. Very often these children appear to have died and then been reincarnated relatively quickly, so they remember and recognize members of their previous families when they see them. They are able to provide personal details and facts that are known only to the previous family, and often show an uncanny ability to speak their family's dialect or immediately find the way to the family house, even though they are in a strange location. As the children grow older, sometimes they forget all the details of their previous family and settle into their "new" family life. Others always keep in touch with their previous family, which can cause jealousy within their current family.

Why do we forget?

A great many cases of reincarnation have been documented and verified by Professor Ian Stevenson, who is a pioneer in this research. If they are true, the implication is that we have all lived before. In that case, surely we should all remember our previous lives?

It may be that many of us do, in subtle ways to which we may not pay much attention. The woman who has always longed to visit Japan, and whose home is full of Japanese artifacts, may be remembering a previous incarnation in that country. The little girl who picks up a violin and immediately knows how to play it may be experiencing strong memories from a previous life in which she was a skilled violinist. The tourist who visits a foreign city for the first time and inexplicably knows his way around it without help of a guidebook might also be tapping into a previous life.

Perhaps the main reason that we don't usually remember our previous lives is because (as in the case of the Indian children) the memories of previous lives cause so much disruption and confusion. We are meant to experience our current lives to the full and not still be caught in the memory of a previous existence.

Reincarnation is accepted much more readily in the East than it is in the West.

Easy and difficult relationships

It would be naïve to expect that a soulmate relationship is always easy-going.

Life would be so simple if we always had harmonious relationships with our soulmates. It would help us to identify them, and we could content ourselves with the knowledge that soulmate relationships are always enjoyable and easy. However, it doesn't always happen like that.

Very often we have a soulmate who loves us so much that she is willing to have a difficult relationship with us. She may even be willing for us to hate her during our current lifetime, as an opportunity for us to learn important lessons about forgiveness and unconditional love. That is why our most problematic relationships are often those that bring us the most development and growth.

LEARNING FROM RELATIONSHIPS

Of course, this doesn't mean that all soulmate relationships should be difficult. They are often enjoyable, satisfying and enriching. But they aren't always smooth sailing. If you think about this, you will realize how important it is to be mentally stimulated and sometimes challenged by other people. Conversely, if you're with someone who agrees with everything you say, it might be pleasant at first, but your conversation will soon become boring. You won't learn anything from it, whereas you will learn a great deal from the person who argues with you, demands that you qualify what you say or encourages you to laugh at yourself. It is the same in long-term relationships. You don't have to reach the stage of throwing plates at each other to have a lively and satisfying relationship.

FIRST MEETINGS

When you meet someone for the first time, your reaction will give you clues about whether this person is a soulmate. You may feel that you know one another already, and start chatting as though you're old friends. You might even fall in love at first sight, which could be another clue that you're repeating a former relationship. Alternatively, you might instantly dislike someone without having any justification for your feelings, yet your relationship may develop despite this, leaving you wondering what is happening. You could have powerful dreams about a person, or see someone else in his face, almost as though you are looking at his previous identity.

KEEPING UP THE CONNECTION

Sometimes problems arise between soulmates because they remember their previous connection, even though it isn't appropriate in their current lives. For instance, two soulmates who were lovers in previous lives might agree in advance, while on the soul planes, that they will only be friends in their next incarnations. However, the bond between them may be so strong or so familiar that, when they meet again on earth, they mistake what was intended to be friendship for love. They might both be married to other people, and so their intense emotional connection creates difficulties that weren't meant to happen.

Other emotions can linger from a previous incarnation and be transferred to the next. One example is the clinging mother who is reluctant to let her child out of her sight, even when he's an adult with his own family. It may be that he was killed in front of her in their previous incarnation together, and on some level she has never forgotten this.

Happily, not all soulmate contacts cause problems. Very often they bring joy, laughter and comfort as two old friends, who have spent lifetimes together, meet up again. They may not necessarily spend much time together, but the link between them will be very deep and significant for both of them. One example is the powerful connection that often exists between a grandparent and grandchild. The grandparent may have agreed in advance to live long enough to be with the grandchild as she grows up, to keep a loving eye on her. When the grandparent dies, he continues to watch over his beloved grandchild in spirit. He might even be her guardian angel (see pages 260–261), who incarnated expressly to guide her through her childhood.

Your relationship with some soulmates in a particular lifetime may only be fleeting.

Understanding the relationship

Soulmate relationships are rarely all bad or all good. They usually fall somewhere in the middle. You might be closely connected to a particular soulmate, even though you don't see him very often. Or you may see him every day, and find it difficult to be civil because he annoys you so much.

THE BIGGER PERSPECTIVE

Although it might be tempting to believe that soulmates only ever have happy relationships, or that you should abandon any close relationships at the first sign of trouble, you need to look at the whole picture. Remember that soulmates have incarnated with you in order to help your soul grow and mature. This means they may have agreed with you, in your between-life states, to cause you problems. So, if the partner who you thought would be your lifelong soulmate suddenly announces that he's leaving you for someone else, you will experience a wide range of entirely human emotions. But you

should also consider, when you feel ready to do so, that this betrayal may have been agreed between the two of you while you were on the soul planes, between lives.

Equally, you should look at a difficult soulmate relationship from the other person's perspective. You might find this person hard to handle, but they may feel exactly the same about you! Once again, you may have agreed in your between-lives state that you would cause problems for this person, perhaps by being demanding, jealous or clingy. Once you begin to understand the many ramifications of soulmate relationships, you realize that it's impossible to judge what goes on between two people because you have no idea what they agreed while on the soul planes. From our human, earthly perspective, a relationship might be abusive or destructive; from our spiritual

Abelard and Heloise's doomed love affair is thought to be a soulmate relationship.

viewpoint, however, two soulmates might have made a tremendous sacrifice by devoting their current lifetimes to tormenting each other.

PAST-LIFE REGRESSION

One way to unravel the mystery surrounding a difficult relationship—especially if it's having a serious impact on your life—is to undergo a past-life regression. This is a technique in which someone who is skilled in conducting regression puts you into a state of light trance and gently encourages you to relive a previous life. This will invariably take you back to a scene in which you were with the person who is causing so much difficulty, and you can see the relationship that existed between you. It might be one of master and slave, or husband and wife, but it will show you some of the shared experiences that link you and explain why your current relationship is so troubled. Please note that this isn't a game, and must only be undertaken by a practitioner who has been trained and knows exactly what she's doing.

There is much debate about whether these regressions really do take you back to previous incarnations or whether

they are merely examples of how vividly your imagination can work. The fact is that it really doesn't matter whether the regressions are real or symbolic, because they provide answers that satisfy the person who is being regressed. Problems are resolved and often the relationship difficulty melts away because the person who has been regressed reaches a greater understanding of her link with her soulmate.

UNRELEASED VOWS

When soulmate connections cause problems, it is often because of unreleased vows that were made between the two people in a previous life. For instance, they might have sworn to love one another for all eternity. However, they forgot to revoke those vows when they reached their between-life state, so these were still operating in their next earthly relationship. However, this time those vows might have been inappropriate because the two people had an entirely different connection, such as teacher and pupil.

Regression may help you to understand the dynamics between you and a soulmate.

Breaking free of a relationship

The cleansing power of fire will help you to break off all contact with a soulmate.

If you realize that you're in a troubling soulmate relationship, how can you break free of it? One way is to look at it clearly, from all angles, preferably with the help of someone who is skilled in past-life work. You will then gain a much broader understanding of the dynamics between you and your soulmate, so that you can find a way round the problem. However, you must make sure that you haven't simply fallen into the trap of thinking that all soulmate relationships are meant to be perfect.

BURNING LETTERS

If you really want to sever your connection with a soulmate, you can burn any letters or cards that you have received from him. Do this in a special ceremony, so that you really feel the connection between you is cleansed by the flames. If you still have his e-mails, print them out and burn them too.

Karma

You may even be able to transform your relationship with this person and therefore transmute much of the karma that still exists between you. Karma is the immutable law of cause and effect and so, very simply, it means that if you're unkind to someone, they will be unkind in return or you will receive the same treatment from a third party. You reap what you sow, and therefore the love and affection that you show to others will also be returned to you.

You must never forget that you're accruing karma all the time and that if you treat someone badly, you will eventually have to deal with the consequences of your actions, either later in this life or next time around. Once you know that, you might be happy to find a compromise with the soulmate who is causing you so much trouble, or you might view the relationship from her perspective. Perhaps she finds you equally difficult? Or maybe she is struggling to overcome an unhappy childhood or other harsh experience. You should also consider that if you're experiencing a troublesome relationship with a soulmate, you are probably reenacting some form of conflict between you from a previous life. If you want to avoid going through it all again in a future incarnation, you must resolve the problem now in the most compassionate way you can imagine.

Cutting your psychic bonds

If you have reached the stage in a close relationship where you seem to be hurting one another more than anything else, or you have reached an impasse with someone, it can be very helpful to cut the psychic cords that exist between you. You might be convinced that you're soulmates or you may not be sure—that doesn't matter. What is important is recognizing that there is a problem between you and doing something about it. This cord-cutting exercise is highly effective if you feel that you can't talk to each other, or if talking has got you nowhere.

Cord-cutting won't destroy the love and affection that exist between you. You will simply be cutting any bonds that seem to be obstructing your relationship or holding it back, or which you feel are inappropriate. This is a healthy exercise to conduct occasionally in any close relationship, even if it isn't problematic. You will soon notice an improvement in your rapport. Be prepared to repeat the exercise at a later date, so that you can once again cut any inappropriate cords.

Choose a time for this meditation when you can be alone and won't be disturbed. It is very important not to lose your attention and focus during this exercise.

Always make sure that you perform any cord-cutting properly. Don't rush through it.

CORD-CUTTING MEDITATION

1 Sit quietly and peacefully, then balance and ground yourself (see pages 24–25).

2 Picture yourself in a favorite place in nature, and know that you are completely safe there. There is a path ahead of you, so walk along it. You will come to a gate. Open the gate, walk through it and close it behind you. You will enter an area that feels very peaceful.

3 Create a circle of protective light around yourself, wide enough to enclose you even when you stretch out your arms.

4 Mentally draw another circle of light a short distance away from you. When you are ready, invite the other person into this circle.

5 When he has arrived, spend time talking to him lovingly about the difficulties between you. Explain that you will not be cutting any ties of unconditional love between you.

6 Begin to notice the cords that link you together, and especially those that look challenging or problematic. For instance, one cord might consist of barbed wire, suggesting an inability to get close to one another, or of padlocks, suggesting control.

7 Sever each cord in the middle, using a pair of silver scissors, then gently pull the cord out of your body and throw it into the space between your two circles. Seal the area of your body with white light. Now repeat the process for the other person, taking care to seal the relevant area of his body with white light, too.

8 Keep cutting the cords. Don't miss any, such as those growing out of your back. Each time you remove a cord from your bodies, be sure to seal the area with white light.

9 When all the ties have been removed, set light to them so that they can be transmuted into positive energy. Draw near to the flames and, if you dare, walk through them, knowing that you won't be harmed.

10 Invite the other person to do the same, but don't force him. Thank him for his cooperation in your meditation, then let him leave. See him go.

11 Walk out of your protective circle and back down the path, then through the gate, taking care to shut it behind you.

12 Count backwards from five. With each number, you are gradually becoming more alert and aware of your surroundings. By the time you have counted down to one, you are completely awake and alert, and are back in your chair.

13 Open your eyes, stretch your arms and legs, and wiggle your fingers and toes.

Finding your soulmate

"The moment I saw him I knew I'd been searching for him all my life." "It was an immediate reaction. Neither of us said a word." These are the sorts of comments you hear when people describe meeting their soulmate. It is generally thought that we all meet several soulmates in our lives. However, they won't all be lovers or partners. Some of them will be friends, relatives or colleagues. Others may be enemies. But for many people there is only one person they want to meet: their romantic soulmate, the person with whom they feel completely at home. So what do you if you can't find your soulmate?

Sometimes we seem to recognize a soulmate the moment we meet him or her.

Why are you looking?

If you're searching for your soulmate without success, one important question to ask yourself is why you want to find him:

• Many people say they feel incomplete without their soulmate. While this is an understandable response, it also raises questions about your sense of self-worth, your wholeness and your relationship with yourself.

• Expecting other people to provide the answer to your problems or to make you feel complete will never work. You need to feel complete in yourself, and therefore happy, before you can make anyone else happy. Otherwise it's like looking for a bandage to stick over a gaping wound in your psyche.

• You may have had a string of difficult relationships in which you always repeat the same patterns, yet be unaware that you may be partly responsible for these relationships not working out as you want.

• You may also be confused between a soulmate, who comes into your life to help you grow and develop (not always a comfortable experience), and a twin flame (see pages 292–293), who is your other half, but whom you may never meet while incarnated on Earth.

• You may be caught up in a romantic dream, like something out of a fairy tale, and believe that your soulmate will rescue you from all your problems.

TALKING TO YOUR GUARDIAN ANGEL

There are several ways to invite your soulmate into your life. The first—and most obvious when you think about it—is to ask. If you work with your guardian angel (see pages 260–261), you should chat to him about your need to find your soulmate. Listen carefully to what he tells you or, if your relationship doesn't work like that, note the signals, situations and dreams that come to you after your conversation. Guardian angels can talk to one another, if asked to do so by the humans they look after, so you could ask your guardian angel to find the guardian angel of your soulmate, and for them to join forces to bring the two of you together.

INVOKING A HIGHER POWER

Another option is to invoke the help of an archangel or ascended master (see pages 270–281). You can either ask for the most appropriate spirit to respond to your request, or you can make contact with Archangel Chamuel, the angel of loving relationships. A host of angels work with him, and they will help you to find your soulmate. Chamuel assists in finding anything that's lost, whether it's a physical object, a loved one or a relationship. When you ask him for help, trust that he is with you and that he will respond to your call. Be patient, and know that your soulmate will arrive in your life at the right time for you both.

WRITING A WISH LIST

Most of us think about what we want to happen in our lives, but don't actually write down our requests. Yet the very act of putting our needs down on paper increases their ability to attract whatever we've asked for. It therefore makes sense to write a profile of the soulmate you want to find. Ideally you should avoid going into too much physical detail in case you become so focused on finding someone who matches that description that you ignore your soulmate, who may look completely different, when she arrives in your life. Instead, concentrate on her qualities and personality, and on the sort of relationship you wish to have with her. Always ask that your relationship will be for the highest good of all concerned.

Writing a list of the preferred traits of your soulmate can attract him into your life.

When you have finished writing your soulmate profile, leave it in a safe place and trust that your request will be granted at the right time. You can read it every now and then, but don't get so caught up in it that you ignore the rest of your life. You never know when or where you might meet your longed-for soulmate. It could be at the party you didn't want to go to, at the supermarket when you're in a hurry or at the bus stop.

CREATIVE DAYDREAMING

Daydreaming may have been frowned upon by your schoolteachers, but it's a highly effective way of attracting what you want into your life. Why not daydream about meeting your soulmate? Let your intuition guide you. When you meet your soulmate in your daydreams, let your whole body be filled with love and exhilaration. This will help to attract him into your life. Your unconscious can't tell the difference between imagination and reality, which is why your heart races when you watch

Daydreaming activates your unconscious so it will start to attract the things you want.

a film in which someone is in peril. You can turn this to your advantage by telling your unconscious that a wished-for event has already happened. It responds by attracting that event and making it happen.

LETTING IT HAPPEN

Whichever route you decide to follow, you must let the entire process happen without any interference on your part. Admittedly that can be difficult if you absolutely long to find this person. However, the sheer force of your longing might actually work against you, because you will be trying too hard and may unwittingly repel the person you're hoping to attract. You must also avoid conflicting emotions, such as thinking, "I wish he'd hurry up and arrive. Maybe he'll never come. He must! Or will I always be alone?" Sending out such confused messages will blur the power of your intentions. You will also be sending out messages about the lack of this person in your life, so you will be attracting even more lack. Focus on what you want, know that you will receive it and be grateful in advance for what you have received.

Psychic pets

Are pets psychic?

If you have ever owned a pet, you will probably have noticed how your animal responds to what's happening at home. Even before you have started to pack your suitcases for a holiday, your pet will somehow know that you're going away and will start to give you reproachful or anxious looks. This is especially likely if your pet will be spending the holiday in a cattery or kennel. Pets also know when we're feeling sad or unwell, and will immediately come to comfort us.

IS THERE ANY EVIDENCE?

Many pet owners have ample evidence that their pets are psychic, although they may hesitate to say it in so many words. This is often through fear of ridicule, although they will happily open up if you ask them about their pet's psychic abilities. For instance, a friend might say that he always knows when you're about to arrive because his dog rushes to the front door to greet you several minutes before you appear.

Maybe the dog doesn't do this for other people, which is what tells your friend that you're on your way.

ANIMAL COMMUNICATION

Imagine what it would be like if you were continually trying to talk to someone you lived with, but she never listened. Instead she told you what to do and always ignored your responses, often not even paying much attention to your behavior. You would be very frustrated by her failure to get the message.

This is how our pets feel, according to people who specialize in psychic communication with animals. They say that our pets try to make contact with us all the time, but usually have little success. Pets realize that we aren't ignoring them because of indifference—it's simply that we don't know how to listen because we communicate in different ways. It doesn't help that many of us have been brought up to believe that it's impossible to talk to animals. But it isn't.

Forget about the concept of so-called dumb animals. They have great intelligence.

Making contact with your pet

If you want to make contact with your pet, it's a lot easier than you think. However, as with all the other techniques in this book, you must train yourself to listen to your intuition and your inner guidance. You might receive the messages that your pet is sending you in the form of words, pictures, sensations or smells. Sometimes your pet might communicate with you when

Dogs are very responsive when you start to communicate with them.

blanking out messages that you don't want to hear because they make you uncomfortable or guilty. For instance, you might become defensive if your rabbit tells you that he doesn't like it when your toddler pulls his tail; or annoyed when your guinea pig announces that she hates her water bottle. However, these are important messages and, if you take note of them, you will start to improve the quality of your pet's life.

FIRST STEPS

When you start to communicate with your pet, ideally you should be sitting near her so that you can observe her behavior. This will give you more clues about the messages she's sending you. At this point, it helps to understand a little about how your pet's species likes to communicate—you will find some detailed information on the next few pages. This will enable you to interpret your pet's body language in the same way that she does when communicating with other members of her species. Use the same basic guidelines for any other animals that you may have as pets.

When your cat meows at you, imagine the message she's giving you.

you're asleep, in the form of dreams.

The precise form of communication doesn't matter—it's what you do with it that's important. So do your best to receive the information from your pet with an open mind and not to question it or tell yourself that it's all your imagination. Don't get caught up in thoughts about how impossible it is that your pet can talk to you; simply trust that it is so. You should also avoid

Your cat's body language

Understanding your cat's body language will help you to know what he's saying to you and how he responds to what you say to him. You will also know if he's feeling peaceful or aggressive.

YOUR CAT'S TAIL

Watch your cat's tail to find out if he's happy. In normal circumstances, a tail that's held up straight is the sign of a contented cat: he's showing that he's friendly and that he recognizes you as a friend. A tail that curves over his back indicates a very happy cat. When his tail flicks from side to side it shows that he's feeling indecisive (especially if he licks his lips at the same time), and when it swishes to and fro very fast it means that he's highly agitated. A bristly tail with all the hairs standing on end (making it look bigger than it really is) indicates extreme defensiveness.

YOUR CAT'S EARS

Your cat's ears also give you a wealth of information. When he's relaxed, his ears point forward and slightly outwards. When alert, his ears prick up and point

The kink in the top of this cat's tail shows that she's happy and contented.

straight ahead. When he's anxious, his ears are erect and twitching. When he's feeling defensive, he completely flattens his ears back against his skull to keep them out of harm's way. When he's aggressive, he flattens his ears, but they are still visible from the front.

YOUR CAT'S WHISKERS

T. C. Lethbridge was a notable dowser (see pages 166–171) and a British scientist who believed that a cat's whiskers act like divining rods, enabling him to tune into his surroundings and read what's there. His whiskers are certainly highly sensitive and help him to sense his surroundings in the dark. When relaxed, your cat holds his whiskers sideways and fairly close together. When alert, his whiskers are fanned out and point forward. When he's defensive, he bunches up his whiskers and presses them against his cheeks.

This cat is showing its stomach, which is always a sign of trust.

Your dog's body language

Dogs like to know where they come in the family pecking order. They usually regard their owners as the top dogs and this is the way it should be: your dog will cause havoc, and could potentially be dangerous, if she thinks she's the top dog in the family. It is difficult to be as precise about a dog's body language as it

This dog's pricked-up ears show that it's interested in what's going on around it.

is about a cat's, because different breeds of dog behave in different ways. Nevertheless, there are still some general pointers that will tell you how your dog is feeling.

SUBMISSION

Because of their need to know who is top dog, dogs can be very submissive. You will know when your dog is behaving like this because she will drop her head and lower her eyes. Her tail will be pressed between her legs. She may even roll over on to her back, revealing her vulnerability by exposing her stomach. She will do this when she knows she's upset you. You might look on this as her attempt to apologize to you.

FEAR

When your dog is frightened, she will behave in a variety of ways. She may become very agitated and restless, barking loudly or being reluctant to leave your side. The pupils of her eyes will dilate, she will flatten her ears against her head and put her tail between her legs.

PRAISE AND LOVE

All the clichés we hear about dogs are true: they are loyal, faithful and affectionate. Dogs are skilled in the art of showing unconditional love and they deserve to receive it from us. Praise your dog when necessary and tick her off the moment she's done something wrong. Your dog won't understand what's happening if you go into a sulk after she's chewed your newspaper. Always showing love for your dog will encourage her to relax with you and will increase the psychic flow between the two of you.

Dogs bark for any number of reasons.

Your horse's body language

Even if you don't own a horse yourself, a little knowledge about equine body language will help you to make easier contact with any horses that you meet.

YOUR HORSE'S EARS

Look at a horse's ears to determine his mood. When his ears gently point upwards and slightly outwards, he's relaxed. When they flop forwards, he's tired or submissive. When they're flattened back against his head, you need to watch out because he's feeling aggressive. If his ears twitch, he's anxious and possibly even frightened. His eyes may also be rolling—a sign that he is unnerved and could lash out.

YOUR HORSE'S TAIL

As you might imagine, when your horse holds his tail high, he's in a good mood and feeling alert. When his tail is tucked between his legs, he's showing submission, fatigue or illness. If he swishes his tail back and forth, he may be flicking away flies, but alternatively he might be annoyed, bad-tempered and angry.

YOUR HORSE'S HEAD

Obviously if your horse reacts to you with open lips and bared teeth, you

This horse's ears and gentle facial expression show that it's feeling relaxed.

Is this horse being playful or aggressive? Its flattened ears suggest the latter.

know this isn't the best time to approach him because he's feeling aggressive. This is emphasized if he's also pawing the ground. However, if he's gently nudging you with his nose, while keeping his mouth closed, he's asking you to give him some affection or an edible treat. The position of his head will tell you a lot about his mood, too. If his head is up (and so is his tail) and he's looking interested in the world around him, he's relaxed and confident. If his head (and tail) is sagging, he's feeling despondent, listless or ill.

HORSEY COMPANY

Horses are sociable animals. In the wild they live in herds and any horse will miss this if he's kept in a field by himself. He will need plenty of human contact to keep him happy and to compensate for the loss of equine company. Alternatively, he will bond with another animal, such as a dog or goat, if he gets the chance.

Horses are such large creatures that it's only wise to pay close attention to their behavior.

Psychic pets

There are some remarkable stories about the psychic ability of pets. Dr. Rupert Sheldrake has studied many cases and his results are fascinating. It seems that animals are immensely sensitive to what is happening to their owners, no matter where those owners happen to be. Dr. Sheldrake has documented cases of animals that rush to the phone whenever their owners ring home, but completely ignore the ringing telephone at all other times. There are stories of pets that have become separated from their owners, but have traveled through unfamiliar territory (sometimes across many miles) to find

If you have a cat, look for signs that suggest it knows when someone is about to come home.

them again. There are also cases of pets that instinctively knew the moment their owners died, even though they were far away from them at the time.

When you read these accounts you may realize that your pet also behaves like this. Animals are tuned into psychic wavebands of which their owners may be ignorant.

ANIMALS AND GHOSTS

Animals can see things that humans can't necessarily detect, such as ghosts. If you live with a pet, you may have noticed that sometimes your pet is watching something you can't see. Your pet may be following the antics of a spider or fly, which is too small for you to detect, but you will usually realize this when your pet pounces on the insect. At other times you may decide there is a less prosaic explanation for your pet's behavior, especially if your pet always reacts like this in a particular area of a room, but nowhere else.

Different animals react in different ways to these unseen forces. Dogs tend to raise their hackles and bark, growl or whimper. Cats, on the other hand, become completely still and alert.

Dogs become very agitated when they're in the presence of a spirit or ghost.

Horses tend to rear up and whinny to show their alarm. When this happens, you could tune into the atmosphere as well, to sense what your pet is seeing.

GHOST PETS

If you love your pet, he becomes part of the family and you will mourn him when he dies. However, that may not be your last contact with him, because there are many stories of dead pets who come back to visit their owners. For example, you might sense your dog jump on to the end of your bed, or feel your cat weaving around your legs, even though she's died. Sometimes this happens years after the pet's death. Alternatively, your cherished pet might return to you reincarnated in another animal's body. When this happens, the new pet will prove its identity by behaving in the same idiosyncratic way as your previous animal. For instance, if your dog used to enjoy playing with a particular toy, but spurned all the others, your new pet might behave in exactly the same way.

The loving bond between an adored pet and its owner remains unbroken by death.

Pets that help their ill owners

If you have a pet, you may have noticed that he seems to sense when you're feeling ill or sad, and shows his support by comforting you in some way. Dogs, with their sensitive and loyal natures, are particularly good at helping their owners in times of crisis. There have been several documented cases of dogs, rabbits and cats that alert their epileptic owners a few minutes before they have a fit. Having been warned, the owner is less likely to hurt herself during her seizure. Although the most likely explanation of such behavior is that the pet has observed minute changes in his owner's actions or smell immediately before the seizure, in some cases the animal is in another room and will suddenly come running.

Some specialist charities are now training dogs to alert their owners in this way. There are even plans to train dogs to detect cancer in patients, after some owners discovered that they had skin cancer only after their dogs kept licking the offending area and thereby drawing their attention to it.

Talking to your pet

Ideally you should create a loving bond with your pet when she first comes to live with you. Spend plenty of time playing with her and stroking her, so that she knows you're friendly and she can trust you. Humans and animals alike enjoy knowing that we're appreciated, so you should repeatedly praise your pet. Tell her how beautiful, clever, loving or brave she is. Tell her you're thrilled to have her in your life. Tell her you love her, and keep saying it. Never tell her she's stupid or lazy, even as a joke, because she won't like it. Neither would you.

PROBLEM-SOLVING TOGETHER

It's wonderful to learn to talk to your pet. It's also very helpful when you're puzzled or annoyed by his behavior. If you give him the chance, he'll tell you what's wrong and then you might be able to do something about it. For instance, if he's reluctant to go into the garden, he might explain that it's because next-door's cat keeps ambushing him. If he's gone off his food, he might tell you that it doesn't taste the way it used to and he'd like to try something else. Or maybe you have recently given him a new food bowl and he doesn't like it. Always treat him like the intelligent creature he is. Apologize to him if necessary, or give a sensible, rational explanation if you can't make the changes he'd like. Don't patronize your pet or behave like a domestic dictator.

LONG-DISTANCE CONVERSATION

You can repeat this conversational process whenever you're separated from your pet. It's especially helpful if you're away from home and you want to check that your pet is all right. For instance, if you're worried that your dog is fretting while you are out shopping, you can send him telepathic messages to say that you will be home soon.

Always act swiftly on any promises that you've made to your pet.

STRIKING UP A CONVERSATION

Choose a time when you're relaxed. Ideally you should have your pet with you and in an equally relaxed mood. Turn off the television or radio, so that there are no external voices to distract you or plant any subconscious ideas in your head.

1 Start by considering what it must be like to your pet. Imagine that you're the same size, with the same fur, feathers or skin. Imagine yourself standing on all fours, if that's how your pet stands (if he's a snake, imagine what that must be like). Consider the following questions:
• What does the world look like from your pet's perspective?
• What does it smell like?
• How much can you see?
• Is the world friendly or full of potential hazards?

• Are you worried about big human feet stepping on you?
• Is your litter tray unpleasantly close to your food?

Spend as much time on this part of the exercise as you need. It may give you some valuable information about how you can improve your pet's life.

2 Now strike up a loving conversation with your pet. You can either do this out loud or in your head. Start by saying hello, in exactly the same way that you'd talk to another human. Ask your pet how he is. Listen to the answer that pops into your head or wait for an image to come to you, and trust it. Don't try to censor or analyze it. Explain to your pet that you're teaching yourself to communicate with him and you'd be delighted if he could help you.

3 Ask him any questions that you like. If he's having behavioral problems, ask him what's wrong, but don't do this in a judgemental way. Listen to his answer. Discuss the situation with him and work out together how you can improve it.

4 When the conversation is over, thank him for talking to you. Tell him that you'd like to chat to him more often.

5 Now you must put your words into action, if necessary. For instance, if you promised to change his food, you must do this as quickly as possible.

Lost pets

If your pet is lost, try to imagine what it may be doing. Is it in a favorite hiding place?

Sometimes a pet can go missing. This might be a dog that dashes off when she's let off her leash or a cat that goes wandering off. As your pet's owner, you will want to know that she's all right and that she'll be home soon. You can alert your neighbors, of course, or even notify the police, but there is no need to feel helpless, because you can also communicate with your pet to find out exactly where she is.

ASKING FOR ANGELIC HELP

In addition to asking for human help, you can also invoke angelic help (see pages 258–273). This can have remarkable results. If you have already established a strong rapport with a particular angel, you can ask him to come to your aid. Alternatively, you can ask Archangel Raphael for help, as one of his specialities is finding lost pets. Another option is to ask your pet's guardian angel to intervene and send her home to you. Always thank the angels for their help.

Pets and the afterlife

When the time comes for your pet to die, this doesn't mean that you lose all communication with him. Although it would hold back his spiritual progress and upset him greatly to burden him with your grief, there is no reason why you can't make contact with him occasionally to say hello. You can do this through a medium, if you wish, or you can connect with him yourself. Sit quietly and think of your pet with love. Say his name and send him a message, such as telling him that you love him and that you hope he's happy. Wait for his answer, which may come to you as an image, an emotion, a physical sensation, a smell or some words either at the time or afterward.

TRACKING YOUR LOST PET

Before you start this exercise, do your best to be calm and balanced. If you aren't, you will be too agitated to concentrate on the messages you're receiving. It may help to take a couple of drops of a flower remedy: try the Bach Flower Remedies of mimulus, for fear; red chestnut, for undue anxiety about your pet; and Rescue Remedy because it's an emergency.

1 Once again, imagine that you're the size and shape of your pet. If she's a cat or dog, imagine that you have got a furry face and whiskers, too. Say her name, either aloud or mentally, and send her love, which will help to establish contact with her.

2 Ask her if she's okay. Wait for an answer. It might come as a feeling, such as a sense of relief and reassurance. You might get a verbal reply. Or you might receive an image. If you immediately get the image of an enclosed space, such as your garage or workshop, your pet may have been accidentally shut in there, so you should go and investigate. If you visualize your local park, go there to see if you can find her.

3 Trust your intuition and the messages that your pet is sending you. If you can't get any visual signs of her whereabouts, but you have a sense of her, ask her to come home because you're worried about her and want to know that she's safe. If she has run away, ask her why.

4 Whether or not you make telepathic contact with your pet, visualize her returning home to you safe and sound. Keep picturing your reunion and how happy you will feel when you see her again. Hold this thought, because it will act like a magnet if your pet is able to return to you.

5 Don't be despondent if this exercise doesn't produce any results at first. Perhaps your anxiety is blocking your pet's telepathic communication. Pay attention to your dreams, too. Many owners have successfully dreamed of the exact location of their missing pet.

Directory of
psychic skills

Different psychic skills

In this section you will find descriptions of various psychic skills, ranging from clairaudience, which is the art of hearing disembodied voices, to psychokinesis, in which objects move or change with what appears to be a life of their own.

KNOWING WHAT'S WHAT

Sometimes it's difficult to know where one skill ends and another begins, or whether they're working together. How, for instance, can you tell the difference between clairvoyance and telepathy? Is a clairvoyant medium, or sensitive, actually seeing messages that are being transmitted to her by discarnate spirits or is she really reading her subject's mind? One simple way to discern this is if the medium recounts facts of which the subject is completely ignorant, but which are later verified by a third party, or if she describes events that have yet to happen and which are not even a possibility at the time of the reading. Another question you might like to ask is whether it is essential to attach specific labels to all these different

Experiment to discover which psychic skills suit you best.

psychic skills. You might prefer to think of them as different facets of the same basic skill, which is the ability to know or detect something through the use of your sixth sense.

SOMETHING FOR EVERYONE

As you explore these different skills you will inevitably discover that you have a greater affinity for some than for others. For instance, you might struggle to practice psychokinesis, but find that you're highly skilled at psychometry. Alternatively, in common with many mediums, you may go through phases in which you're successful at using a particular skill and then lose that ability, but become skilled at something else. It's as though you're being given the chance to test out each skill until you find the one at which you excel.

When you work with these psychic skills, always keep an open mind and be prepared to learn from your mistakes. Don't be afraid to admit that sometimes you may get things wrong. No one— not even the most experienced medium —is correct all the time.

Be patient when developing your skills.

Clairvoyance

Clairvoyance is often used as an umbrella term for other forms of psychic skill, yet it is really very specific and means "clear seeing." This includes being able to see spirit entities either as a physical manifestation (as though live humans were standing in front of you) or vividly with your mind's eye (as

Clairvoyance is the art of seeing with your psychic vision.

though you're mentally watching a film). So if you can actually see spirits, rather than simply hear or sense them, you are clairvoyant.

MORE THAN ONE GIFT

Clairvoyants usually have more than one psychic gift. For instance, they may be clairaudient as well, so they can hear what the spirits are saying to them; or they might be clairsentient, so they can physically experience the sensations the spirit is trying to convey. Having two or more psychic gifts enables them to make greater contact with spirits and thereby increases the chances of them correctly interpreting the messages that the spirits are trying to convey.

FAITH AND PATIENCE

One of the best ways to understand how clairvoyance works is to practice it yourself. However, you must be patient and not expect to achieve astonishing results overnight. Such skills usually come with time, patience and pratice. It is also very important to keep hold of the idea that you will eventually succeed, so that you don't give up at the first hurdle.

Interpreting symbols

Receiving spirit messages clairvoyantly isn't always as easy as it sounds. Spirits often communicate using symbols, so the clairvoyant has to decide what these mean before passing on the message. This is one reason why the messages aren't always clear or can take some time to decipher. If the medium is shown a collection of flowerpots, he has to decide how to interpret them. Do they refer to someone who is a gardener, a potter, who works in a garden center or whose name might be Potts?

Physical mediumship

Fashions in mediumship, just as in everything else, come and go. In Victorian times and at the start of the 20th century, physical mediumship (also called materialization) was very popular. It was quite remarkable and, once seen, was never forgotten. A medium would go into a deep trance and then exude a light, silky substance called ectoplasm from her body. This would gradually build up into a spirit form that would then speak to everyone in the room. When people touched the spirit form, they were surprised to find that its hands were warm and solid. The medium would also psychically be the channel for direct voice communications from spirits through ethereal trumpets or other instruments, rappings or psychokinesis, table levitations and apports (objects that have apparently materialized out of thin air). At the end of each sitting, the medium's body would reabsorb the ectoplasm, which looked like very fine muslin.

DECLINE AND DISBELIEF

Although many physical mediums were perfectly genuine, others were not. Each sitting had to be held in a darkened room in order for the ectoplasm to be visible, so it was very tempting for some people to turn this to their advantage. A fraudulent medium could employ someone dressed in swathes of muslin to behave like a spirit. Trumpets were often blown by the medium's assistant or by the medium herself. As a result, this form of mediumship became associated with trickery and fraud. Unfortunately the general assumption seemed to be that if one physical medium was a fake, they all were.

Another reason for the decline of physical mediumship was the danger it presented to the medium. A medium should never be touched while in a trance, as the shock to her system can make her ill for a long time. She was therefore very vulnerable to sitters inadvertently harming her while she was in a trance.

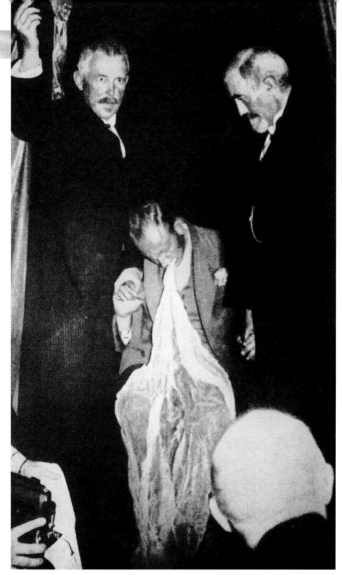

Einer Nielsen was a Danish medium. Here, he is shown secreting ectoplasm from his mouth.

Famous clairvoyants

Many clairvoyant sensitives, or mediums, have become famous, thanks to the accuracy of the evidence they give about the spirits they contact. In most cases they had the gift of clairvoyance from childhood. Originally clairvoyants worked either with private clients or in Spiritualist churches, but in recent years they have become popular on television, which has vastly increased the number of people who are able to watch them work.

ENA TWIGG
Ena Twigg was born in Britain shortly before World War I. She was a trance medium who was clairvoyant and clairaudient. In common with many sensitives, Ena Twigg was psychic throughout her life and as a child used to see spirits, which she called "misty people." She had many successes, but one of the most celebrated was her ability to trace Bishop James Pike, who went missing in the Judean desert in September 1969. At the time no one knew what had happened to him, but in a private sitting Ena Twigg went into a trance and the bishop, who was in a transition phase between life and death, came through very strongly and described the circumstances around his death. These were verified three days later when his body was finally found.

BETTY SHINE
A British clairvoyant, Betty Shine was primarily a healer who wrote books detailing her miraculous healing work. She first made contact with her spirit guide at the age of two, and as an adult was told that she would become a powerful healer with clairvoyant abilities. Although she worked rather reluctantly as a medium, she was always much happier when giving healing. It was during these sessions that she did most of her clairvoyant work by seeing spirit forms building up around her, and by viewing spirits who wanted to contact the patients to whom she was giving healing.

Ena Twigg's clients often commented on how normal and down-to-earth she was.

JOHN EDWARD

An American clairvoyant who first discovered his psychic gift as a toddler, John Edward has become a celebrated sensitive. As a child, he would travel on the astral plane at night and he could also see the auras around people. He thought everyone could do this and that there was nothing special about him. He began to read playing cards and discovered that he knew things about his clients without being told. John Edward has written several books about his work and has also hosted a successful television series.

GORDON SMITH

Dubbed "the psychic barber" because he used to run a barber's shop in Scotland, Gordon Smith is renowned for the quality and accuracy of his work. He is able to give precise names, ages and addresses, as well as a great deal of other highly specific evidence. His first psychic experience took place when he was seven; he saw a family friend walking down the road, apparently just as normal, but then he discovered that the man had died ten days before. Gordon Smith blocked off his psychic abilities until his twenties, when they reasserted themselves and he joined a development circle. He is clairvoyant, clairaudient and clairsentient.

JAMES VAN PRAAGH

James Van Praagh is one of America's most well-known clairvoyants. One of his most celebrated cases happened in June 1995 and involved a young man who died after an accident on Mount Fuji in Japan. James Van Praagh gave the man's parents a tremendous amount of evidence, including details of a photograph taken of him before his death, but which had not, at the time of the sitting, been developed.

Developing clairvoyant skills

Unless you are lucky enough to have an innate clairvoyant gift that is fully active, you will have to develop your skills. There are various ways in which you can do this.

PSYCHIC DEVELOPMENT GROUPS

One of the classic routes is to join a psychic development class, in which you will be guided by someone with plenty of experience in dealing with the spirit world. This person usually has mediumship abilities. If you don't know how to find such a group, you could contact a recognized spiritual organization to see if any groups are operating in your area.

Alternatively, you could start your own psychic circle (see pages 184–191), in which you help one another to develop.

MEDITATION

Meditation (see pages 44–45) is one of the best ways to develop your clairvoyant skills, especially if you practice visualization meditations. These will develop your ability to see images in your mind's eye. This is really your third eye, and it is this brow chakra that enables you to see clairvoyantly. You do this quite naturally when you daydream —you see images in your mind as though they were really happening, blotting out everything around you, and exactly the same thing happens when you're using your clairvoyant skills.

You can create your own visualization meditations. Alternatively, there are many guided meditation tapes and CDs available from noted spiritual teachers.

BOOKS

Many clairvoyants have written books describing their skills (including all the clairvoyants mentioned on pages 346–347). Some of these books contain useful information about how you can develop your own psychic abilities.

Visualization meditation is excellent for strengthening your mind's eye.

YOUR MENTAL TELEVISION SCREEN

Your clairvoyant skills won't develop until you have worked on your brow chakra (see pages 76–77). Here is a good exercise for cleaning and clearing this chakra so that it will work as effectively as possible. At first you should aim to practice this exercise several times a week. Each time it will become easier to use the mental television screen that you have created, and your clairvoyant images will become stronger.

1 Set aside a time when you won't be disturbed. Sit quietly in a comfortable chair, with both feet flat on the floor.

2 Put yourself into a relaxed state, and then ground and balance yourself (see pages 24–25), and surround yourself with a protective bubble of white light (see pages 104–105). Close your eyes.

3 Starting with your base chakra, mentally illuminate each chakra in turn, seeing it as a glowing ball of colored light. When you reach your brow chakra, picture it as a round ball of indigo light. Look closely at this ball. Can you see any darker patches? If so, imagine them dissolving and disappearing. Now mentally light up your crown chakra.

4 Still with your eyes closed, focus on the area between your eyebrows. Imagine that you have a big television screen here. Mentally draw the outline of the screen. Now create a set of buttons that control the size, brightness and sharpness of the images you will be seeing on this screen. Create an on-off switch, too.

5 Imagine yourself polishing the screen with a duster. Clear away any dust, cobwebs or other debris that will obscure the images that will soon

appear on the screen. Keep doing this until the screen is sparkling clean.

6 When you're ready, press the on-off switch to "on." Can you see any images yet? If so, allow them to materialize and take note of them. If not, picture a simple image, such as a tree or a field of waving corn. Sharpen it or increase the brightness using your control buttons. You may not physically see anything on the screen, but you will see it in your mind's eye. Allow the image to become as real and three-dimensional as possible.

7 After a few minutes of looking at this image (and any others that come to you), switch off the screen.

8 Close down your chakras (see pages 188–189) and gently come back to your surroundings.

Clairaudience

If you are clairaudient you have the gift of being able to hear spirit noises, voices and other sounds. You are listening on another level of vibration, and hearing sounds that most people haven't noticed. This is rather similar to dogs, which can hear sounds that are beyond the human range of audibility.

Many sensitives are clairaudient, in conjunction with other mediumistic abilities. For instance, a medium might be clairaudient and clairvoyant, so he can hear and see spirit entities.

HOW CLAIRAUDIENCE WORKS

If you are clairaudient, you either hear sounds inside your head or as though they are outside you. When these sounds are apparently outside you, you may wonder why no one else can hear them. Even when they are inside your head, they may be so loud and definite that it's as though someone has spoken out loud.

If you ever visit a clairaudient sensitive for a sitting, or watch one

working from the platform at a Spiritualist meeting, you will notice that sometimes he has difficulty in hearing what the spirits are saying. That's because spirit communication is not necessarily easy to understand. In order to make contact with the physical world, spirits have to slow down their vibrations quite dramatically, and they can only do this for a certain amount of time before they become tired. As a result, their voices can sound jerky, clipped, speeded up or as though they're being transmitted by a very tinny radio. Sensitives often have difficulty in distinguishing consonants that sound similar. For example, they may not be able to tell whether a spirit's earthly name was May, Kay, Rae or Fay.

DO ALL SPIRITS SPEAK THE SAME LANGUAGE?

Sometimes a clairaudient makes contact with the spirits of people who came from other countries and spoke foreign languages, yet she is able to understand

Clairaudience means "clear hearing." You hear sounds from another vibration.

Sometimes your sleep may be disturbed by the sound of spirits talking or singing.

them very well. You might wonder how this is possible. In fact, each spirit speaks in the language that he knew when on Earth, and this is then translated by outside forces, such as the clairaudient's guides, into a language that she understands. Some clairaudients receive these translations in the form of symbols, while others report hearing the messages translated into their own language. So it seems that the exact way in which this process operates will vary from one clairaudient to the next.

WHAT YOU CAN EXPECT TO HEAR

When you receive a clairaudient message, it can arrive in many different forms. You might hear someone speaking to you, even though no one is around. You might be woken at night by the sound of someone singing, talking or whispering. Alternatively, you could hear music playing. You must of course check that such sounds aren't coming from an earthly source before you consider that they might be clairaudient communications. If you hear music playing, is it coming from the street or your next-door neighbor? Can anyone else in the house hear it? Is it a piece that has special significance for you?

A celebrated clairaudient

Most sensitives with clairaudient gifts are talented in other ways, too. One of the most well known was Doris Stokes, a British clairaudient who traveled the world and gave sittings to many famous people. She was strongly clairaudient, as well as clairvoyant, and in her autobiographies she describes many instances of hearing spirit voices. One of the most joyful experiences for her was hearing a disembodied voice telling her that her husband, who was missing in action and presumed dead during World War II, was actually alive. One of the saddest was being told by the voice that her completely healthy five-month-old son had served his time on Earth and was wanted back in the spirit world; he died from a sudden illness a couple of weeks later. The spirit of his dead father came to collect him.

Developing clairaudient skills

Clairaudience may come to you at the same time as other psychic gifts or it may develop independently of them. Most of us have always had episodes of clairaudience, although we might not have been aware of them. For instance, you might occasionally have heard an inner voice prompting you to do something, or someone calling your name, even though there was no one there.

LISTENING TO THE SILENCE

If you want to increase your powers you must expand your listening skills.

1 Ground and balance yourself as usual (see pages 24–25), and then surround yourself with a protective bubble of white light (see pages 104–105).

2 Put a pair of earplugs in your ears or wear a pair of disconnected headphones. Sit quietly and listen to the noises inside your head.

3 Stop after 20 minutes and write down your experiences in a journal that you keep for this purpose.

4 Ground and balance yourself again, because this exercise can disorientate you. Then protect yourself again with white light.

LISTENING TO A SHELL

One way to enhance your clairaudient skills is to listen to a constant noise, such as the white noise of a radio that has not been tuned into any station. As you listen to the white noise you may hear voices, either coming from the radio or inside your own head. An alternative is to cup a large shell to your ear. The soft whisperings will help to trigger your clairaudience.

1 Ground and balance yourself as usual (see pages 24–25), and then surround yourself with a protective bubble of white light (see pages 104–105).

2 Cup a large shell to your ear and close your eyes. Let your mind settle into the murmurings coming from the shell.

3 Stop after 20 minutes and write down your experiences.

4 Ground, balance and protect yourself again before standing up.

Clairsentience

The gift of clairsentience means "clear feeling," so you experience the sensations and emotions that belong to other people or to spirits as though they're happening to you. Healers often have the ability to feel the pain or discomfort of their patients, and this can guide them to the area of their patient's body that needs healing. When a clairsentient sensitive, or medium, makes contact with a spirit, he will experience the emotions and physical feelings that are transmitted by that spirit. For instance, he might know how the person died because he will experience the same bodily sensations, such as a pain in his chest if the person died from a heart attack.

Clairsentience also enables you to pick up the atmosphere around you, such as when you go into a haunted building and feel uncomfortable or as though someone is watching you. Psychometry, which is explored in greater depth later in this section (see pages 364–369), is another form of clairsentience.

Feeling heat or cold in your aura is an example of clairsentience.

IS IT SIMPLE TELEPATHY?

There are occasions when it's difficult to distinguish between clairsentience and telepathy. For example, there are many stories of the partners of pregnant women who experience all the pains of labor at the same time as the real labor. There are even some cases in which the pregnant woman had no pain at all, but her partner was in agony. All these experiences probably owe more to telepathy than pure clairsentience. Cases in which the people concerned are separated physically and have no means of getting in touch with each other are more suggestive of clairsentience, although they may still be telepathic.

PSYCHIC DETECTIVES

The most convincing examples of clairsentience occur when the person who is experiencing the emotions or physical sensations is doing so "blind," with no prior knowledge of the circumstances involved. For instance, although they don't always advertise the

Psychometry is a classic clairsentient skill. Some psychics use it to trace missing persons.

fact, police forces around the world sometimes call on the help of sensitives when dealing with particularly tricky cases. Some of these sensitives are clairsentient, so they go through the physical sensations that were experienced by the people involved in the cases. If the police are investigating a baffling case of a missing person, for example, they might ask for the help of a clairsentient, who is given one of the possessions belonging to the person for whom the police are searching. The clairsentient is then able to tune into the energy of the missing person and may be able to say what has happened to him, based on her own physical sensations. She might go through all the sensations of death by drowning, or might report that she thinks the missing person is locked up in a small room with shackles on his hands and feet.

SUPERNATURAL SCENTS

When someone dies, his family and friends sometimes experience inexplicable smells that remind them of him. If the person concerned was a smoker, but the rest of the family doesn't smoke, they may suddenly catch whiffs of cigarette smoke for no apparent reason. They might explain these away by thinking that the furniture has become impregnated with the smoke, and that's what they can smell. But that won't explain why the smoke isn't noticeable all the time. It may well be that the spirit of that person is trying to contact his loved ones by sending them a smell with which he was associated. Alternatively, if he was a keen rose-grower, he might send his family the scent of roses. In the summer this could be confused with the scent of roses wafting in from the garden, but it would be another matter in the dead of winter when no roses are in bloom. Many bereaved people report smelling their loved one's favorite aftershave or perfume in the air, especially at important times, such as significant anniversaries. This is a simple form of clairsentience.

There are many instances of people who can smell scents that seem to have no connection with their surroundings, such as smelling the scent of bread baking. This may well be a smell that is brought by a ghost that haunts the property.

Take note of floral scents that arrive out of season, such as the scent of a rose in the winter.

Developing clairsentience

If you want to develop clairsentience you need to become more sensitive to your surroundings, so that you can start to pick up the energies and vibrations around you. There are many different ways to do this, but here are some suggestions. You can also practice psychometry (see pages 364–369), which is an excellent use of clairsentience.

A haunted house

When you conduct this exercise you need to choose a house that is known to be haunted by a particular spirit, without discovering who that spirit is. For instance, you could visit an old house that is open to the public, but without reading the guidebook or listening to the tour guide. Walk through each room in turn, checking to see if you register any sensations or smells that don't belong to you. Do you feel anxious or nervous in one room, but perfectly all right everywhere else? When you have completed your tour of the house you can verify the impressions you received by checking the audio guide or guidebook or by talking to one of the attendants.

WHO'S BEEN SITTING IN MY CHAIR?

2 When the time has elapsed, everyone should stand up and move to the next chair on their left without speaking. You should all sit in your new chair and tune into the energy that you can feel emanating from it.

3 Silently take note of the sensations that come to you. Do you feel any different in this new chair? Do you feel anxious, relaxed, tired, wide awake, sad or happy?

You need to practice this exercise with several other people. Each of you should sit in your own chair in the same room.

1 Everyone should close their eyes. Then you should all either meditate or simply sit quietly in your chairs for about 20 minutes.

4 After a few minutes ask each person in turn to describe their sensations, and ask the person who previously sat in your current chair to comment on them. Very often, this person will verify that the sensations described were experienced by them while sitting in the chair.

Psychometry

Everything—animate and inanimate—has an aura. The more frequently an object is used, the more likely it is to have a strong aura. For instance, a wedding ring is surrounded by an electromagnetic field that contains information about what has happened to it over the years. Its aura can tell us about the people who have worn it and the significant events that have happened to those people. On the other hand, a chair that sits in a spare bedroom may not have such a strong aura, unless something significant has happened near it over the years.

Psychometry is the art of reading the aura of inanimate objects, usually by holding them. You may already do this, without realizing it, whenever you decide not to buy an object in a shop because it doesn't feel right. Imagine that you're attracted to a gold bracelet in the window of an antique shop. You go in and ask to try it on. It looks pretty, but the moment it's on your wrist you start to feel depressed, your head begins to ache or you feel cold or tired. You think this is only a coincidence, but you decide not to buy the bracelet anyway. As you go out of the shop, you see it being replaced in the window. It's odd, you think, because it still looks nice, but for some peculiar reason there's now something about it that you don't like.

In fact, you have just been practicing psychometry. You have tapped into the aura of the bracelet and picked up the energy of one of its previous owners, who may have been depressed or ill. However, you won't be able to confirm this because you're unlikely to discover the history of the bracelet.

WORKING IN A GROUP
A very effective way to practice psychometry is to work with a group of friends who share your aims. This is a particularly good exercise for a psychic

Trust your instincts when picking up the energy of an object. See what comes to you.

circle (see pages 184–191), because your combined energy helps to raise the vibrations in the room and boost everyone's psychic abilities.

Arrange for everyone to bring two or three objects on which to practice psychometry. These objects should be relatively small so that they're easily portable, and they should also have been in close contact with their owner for a long period to ensure that they've picked up their owner's energy. You can choose a wide variety of objects, such as watches, rings, other jewelry, purses, wallets, fountain pens, soft toys and keys, provided that their history is known only by the person who brings them.

Ask everyone to place their objects on a large tray, over which you have laid a cloth so that no one can see the other objects. Gently move the objects around, so that they are well jumbled up. When everyone is ready, either you or the leader of the group should ask each person in turn to choose an object and then practice psychometry on it (see page 364). If necessary, you can set a time limit for each reading. At the end of the readings, encourage everyone to give their constructive feedback.

Small objects worn close to the body, such as watches and pens, are ideal for psychometry.

GIVING A PSYCHOMETRY READING

If you're interested in learning more about psychometry and honing your skills, you must work with objects whose history is known, but not by you. You will then gain valuable feedback about whether your reading is correct. If you know nothing about the history of the object, you won't know whether you're completely accurate or way off the mark until this is revealed to you. This means that you need to work in tandem with someone who can give you a suitable object to read. Choose someone who is positive and open-minded, and with whom you feel comfortable. Ideally the object shouldn't belong to her, so that it won't have picked up her energy. For instance, she could give you her grandmother's wedding ring or her son's watch, without supplying any clues about its ownership.

1 Before you start your reading, make sure that you're grounded and balanced (see pages 24–25) as usual. This will help you to distinguish between your own emotions and physical sensations, and those triggered by the psychometry reading.

2 Now take hold of the object in whichever way you wish and sit quietly with it for a couple of minutes. Close your eyes if this improves your concentration. Breathe normally and let yourself tune into the object you're holding.

3 Some psychometrists like to hold the object loosely in the palms of their hands. Others prefer to touch it with their fingertips, and some people like to hold it against their foreheads. Choose whichever method feels right for you and gives you the best results.

4 Take note of the thoughts, emotions, images or bodily sensations that come to you. Don't attempt to analyze them, and don't worry if they fail to make any sense. Although the impressions that come to you may seem strange or far-fetched, you must always mention them. They may have great significance for the person for whom you're giving the reading. You may see an image of a chicken and wonder what it means. If you aren't sure how to interpret it, simply say that you can see a chicken. It may mean that the owner of the object keeps chickens or lives at Rooster Cottage.

5 Simply start talking and see what happens—this is one of the best ways to give a psychometry reading, especially when you're still learning how to do it. You may hear yourself speaking fluently and wonder how you're getting so much information. Don't let this make you self-conscious. Keep speaking, and say whatever comes into your mind. Stop when you have nothing more to say. Don't start making things up.

6 Now ask the other person to give you some feedback. Encourage her to be honest with you, because it's a waste of time for both of you if she says you were completely accurate when in reality you got little right. However, this is unlikely to happen. It's far more probable that you will be amazed by your high level of accuracy.

Precognition and premonition

There is a subtle difference between premonition and precognition. A premonition literally means "to give prior warning to," whereas precognition means "to know in advance." Therefore, premonitions frequently involve a sense of foreboding.

Humankind has always experienced precognition and premonitions, and most of us are familiar with the feeling that we should or shouldn't do something. There are many cases of people whose intuition told them not to take a particular plane or train, and who were then horrified to learn that it had been involved in a fatal accident. On other occasions people have taken action to avoid their fate and have encountered it anyway. This conjures up questions about our free will and about when we are meant to die. Some people claim that we die at absolutely the right time for us—there are no mistakes about the time and place of our death. Others believe that we have several opportunities to die during our lifetimes and we can choose whether to take them.

HONING YOUR INTUITION

As with all psychic techniques, you can train yourself to become more aware of your intuitive promptings. The best way to do this is to listen and then act on them. You can also write them down in a special journal, noting the premonition, the action you took and the outcome. The trick is to

Forgetting to set your alarm clock may mean that you avoid a fatal accident.

Appointment in Samarra

An old Middle Eastern legend deals with the idea that we are fated to die at a certain time. A servant was shopping in a bazaar in Baghdad when he was horrified to bump into Death. Death fixed the servant with such a penetrating gaze that he rushed back to his master in terror and explained what had happened. He asked to borrow a horse so that he could get out of Baghdad fast and reach Samarra by nightfall. The master agreed and the servant rode off. A little later the master went to the bazaar and saw Death, who was still standing in the crowd. Unafraid, he confronted him and asked him why he'd frightened his servant that morning. "I was surprised to see him here," replied Death. "I have an appointment with him in Samarra this evening."

pay attention to your premonitions without over-analyzing them or becoming overly conscious of them. Simply let them register in your mind and then write them down.

Such premonitions will vary from the mundane to the highly impressive. For example, you might decide to take an umbrella when you go out on a brilliantly sunny day because you're convinced it's going to rain later—and it does. Or you might suddenly become anxious about a friend, convinced that something has happened to her, and later discover that she's broken her leg.

There are some celebrated cases of premonition and precognition, although unfortunately they often end in tragedy.

CHEIRO AND THE *TITANIC*

There are many stories about people who have had forebodings about

There are many cases of premonition about the sinking of the Titanic, *even though she was deemed unsinkable.*

traveling on a particular day or in a particular mode of transport. Before the *Titanic* left Southampton on her maiden voyage to New York on April 10, 1912, there were premonitions that she would sink. The ship was famously described as being unsinkable, so we might imagine that these forebodings were easily dismissed. One person who certainly ignored the warnings was the journalist and editor W. T. Stead. He was worried about being killed by mob violence and consulted Cheiro, the famous palmist, about this several times. In June 1911 Cheiro wrote to Stead telling him that the only danger he faced was from water. He warned Stead to avoid traveling by water, particularly in mid-April 1912, otherwise "you will meet with such danger to your life that the very worst may happen." Stead had a ticket for the *Titanic's* Atlantic crossing and ignored Cheiro's warning. He drowned when the ship hit an iceberg on April 15.

This is a fascinating example of precognition on Cheiro's part. He was renowned for his accuracy, not only in palmistry, but also in numerology and astrology. Stead would have known this, because Cheiro's talents were celebrated on both sides of the Atlantic, yet he still chose to sail on the *Titanic* because he felt duty-bound to do so.

The story raises another question, too. What would have happened to Stead if he'd stayed in London and not sailed on the *Titanic* that April? Would some other danger involving water have befallen him?

THE ASSASSINATION OF ROBERT KENNEDY

Not everyone who has a premonition about disaster befalling another person is able to pass it on to him. One extraordinary example of this is Jeanne Gardner, a housewife from West Virginia.

She had always heard a voice that gave her warnings, and in 1967 the voice told her that Robert Kennedy would be assassinated. A year later, at the start of June, the voice told her that Senator Kennedy would be murdered in a "galley" in the early hours of June 5 by a short man. The message ended with the words "Sirhan Sirhan." Mrs. Gardner was so distraught by this information that on the night of June 4 she blurted it out to many people attending a booksellers' conference in Washington (she had gone there to find a publisher for her autobiography), saying that Kennedy would be murdered in a kitchen early the following morning. Sure enough, Robert Kennedy died a few hours later, having been shot on June 5, 1968 at 12:15 a.m. in the food service pantry at the Ambassador Hotel in Los Angeles, by a short man called Sirhan Sirhan.

Mrs. Gardner's premonition is notable not only for its accuracy and detailed information (including correctly naming Robert Kennedy's assassin), but also for the fact that she announced it to so many witnesses the night before the assassination took place.

Telepathy and ESP

In the 1930s the term "ESP," or extrasensory perception, was adopted as a more scientific alternative to what was commonly called telepathy. While telepathy was frowned upon, ESP was considered to be rather respectable. Dr. J. B. Rhine, one of the great investigators of parapsychology, had coined the phrase "ESP" and carried out many studies at Duke University in North Carolina to discover exactly what this ability was. Today the distinctions between telepathy and ESP tend to be blurred, and the two terms are often used interchangeably. However, this isn't accurate, because there are certain differences between them.

Telepathy describes the transmission of thoughts and emotions from one person's mind to another. ESP, on the other hand, describes the ability to perceive something without using any of the normal five senses. It therefore covers a wide range of skills, including clairvoyance, psychometry, dowsing, telekinesis, remote viewing, precognition and, indeed, telepathy.

PRACTICING TELEPATHY

Most of us have experienced some form of telepathy, although we may have shrugged it off as mere coincidence. An everyday example is when one person says what the other is thinking, especially if this isn't related to what is happening at the time. This occurs especially with people who know one another very well. For instance, a husband and wife might be busily working in their garden one summer's day when the husband starts to think about them going away for Christmas, instead of holding their usual big family celebration at home. A moment later, and before he has had a chance to say anything, his wife puts his thoughts into words and makes the same suggestion herself. Another simple example is thinking about someone and almost immediately receiving a phone call from them. Telepathy is also particularly strong between parents and their children; often a parent will know, without having to be told, that her child is ill or in trouble.

*Telepathic communication is often very strong
between parents and their children.*

EXPERIMENTING WITH TELEPATHY

One of the classic ways to test whether someone has telepathic powers is to use a deck of cards called Zener or ESP cards. This deck of twenty-five cards was developed by Dr. Rhine and named for his associate, Karl Zener. There are five cards each of five different designs: a circle, a cross, a square, a star and some wavy lines. In this forced-choice experiment (so-called because there is no choice about which images are transmitted), one person sends the images on the card to the other person, who sits in a different room.

The cards are shuffled well by the person who will be sending the images, and are then dealt out one by one. The sender of the images concentrates on the first image for two minutes, while the receiver tries to visualize the image and then writes it down. At the end of the two minutes, the sender rings a bell to indicate that he is moving on to the next card. When all twenty-five cards

Zener cards were developed to test a person's powers of telepathy.

have been transmitted, the sender and receiver compare notes. A score of five correctly identified cards is consistent with pure chance. A higher score suggests that telepathy is at work.

SIMPLE ESP TESTS

You can test your ESP in many ordinary situations. For instance, the next time you arrange to meet a friend somewhere, aim to arrive slightly early. Then ask yourself the exact time of your friend's arrival. Listen to the answer and see if you're right. Alternatively, if you are in a restaurant, you can ask yourself how many people will come through the door before your friend appears. Once again, listen to the answer and see if it's correct.

Another simple test is to sense the color of objects. You can easily do this with a small collection of colored felt-tip pens. Arrange the pens in front of you, then close your eyes and move them around so that there is no likelihood of you remembering their exact position. Now either pick up a pen or hold your hand over it and sense its color. Open your eyes to see if you are correct.

Déjà vu

When we experience déjà vu, we feel as though history is repeating itself. We get the most uncanny sensation of intense familiarity, as though we have lived through a particular moment before and are now experiencing it again, even though in reality we're doing it for the first time. Very often this sense of déjà vu occurs over trivial incidents. For example, you might be chatting to a friend in a café about the film you saw recently, and you suddenly feel as though you have done exactly the same thing before, in every detail.

Déjà vu is a French phrase which, translated literally, means "already seen." It happens entirely spontaneously and can't be consciously triggered. Years may go by between episodes.

WHAT IS IT?

There are several theories about déjà vu. Some people regard it as nothing more mysterious than a brain malfunction, in which the brain is briefly unable to detect the difference between the present and the past. Indeed, déjà vu is a recognized symptom of temporal-lobe epilepsy: someone has a strong sense of déjà vu either shortly before or during an epileptic seizure. Another theory states that it is wish fulfillment on the part of the person having the experience, although this doesn't explain why some very mundane situations can trigger a sense of déjà vu. In psychology, the experience is known as paramnesia. Another theory is that déjà vu is related to a past-life experience, and we feel that we've been somewhere before because we have.

I'VE BEEN HERE BEFORE

Although not every experience of déjà vu is likely to be connected to a past life, some are so striking that the theory is definitely worth considering. Several such experiences are recounted by Arthur Guirdham in his book *The Cathars and Reincarnation*, and together they form a convincing argument for reincarnation.

Some experiences of déjà vu are so mundane that it's hard to find a reason for them.

Remote viewing

Wouldn't it be useful to know what was happening on the other side of the world without having to use any special technological equipment? It would enable us to observe loved ones who are far away, and governments would be able to spy on other countries. Such abilities might sound like the stuff of science fiction, but they are already practiced in a technique known as remote viewing. This is a form of clairvoyance, in which someone is given

Big Brother is watching

In today's world we are continually under surveillance by closed-circuit television cameras, satellites and many other devices. And, although we don't realize it, we may also be watched by remote viewers who are trained by governments. In 1995 the U.S. government admitted that it had launched a remote-viewing program in the 1970s, when the Cold War was still raging, that enabled it to spy on Russia and other countries considered to be hostile at the time. This was "Star Gate," which ran until 1995. Various techniques were used, but one of the most successful was to give the remote viewers nothing more than the coordinates of a particular latitude and longitude and ask them what they could see. Their reports were remarkably accurate and detailed. Perhaps remote viewing is still being practiced?

the name of a place somewhere in the world and then asked to describe it. Remote viewers, as they are called, can be remarkably accurate, especially when they give descriptions of sights that they don't understand.

LOOK FOR YOURSELF
If you wish to practice remote viewing yourself, ideally you need a helper to verify what you have seen. This person could supply you with the map coordinates for a place that she already

Remote viewers provide detailed descriptions of the places they can see.

knows, and then give you useful feedback on your viewing experiments. Alternatively, you could view her when she is at home or out and about. Don't agree on a specific time for this viewing, because you will then inevitably be thinking about one another and this may trigger telepathy, which will distort the experiment. However, you may agree on a specific day.

Psychokinesis

Put very simply, psychokinesis (also known as PK) is the ability to exert mind over matter. For instance, this might involve moving a chair across a room. It might sound extraordinary, but there is nothing new about it. There is a notable example of psychokinesis in the Bible, when Jesus Christ changed water into wine.

PK has been investigated thoroughly in scientific laboratories, with varying degrees of success. It requires tremendous mental concentration in most people, but not in others. Some PK practitioners sweat copiously during the experiments and lose pounds in weight, while others, such as Uri Geller, can practice PK effortlessly.

BENDING SPOONS
Uri Geller's ability to bend spoons caused a sensation when it was first publicized on British television in the early 1970s. Perfectly ordinary metal spoons, which had been completely rigid and had behaved in the way you would expect, would soften and then twist themselves into convoluted shapes while Geller stroked them. Although magicians claim this is nothing more than a simple conjuring trick, or that Geller physically bent the spoons when no one was looking, science had a different answer. When Geller's bent spoons were analyzed in laboratories, the metal was found to have been put under extraordinary stress that was not consistent with manual bending. Some other force was at work. Interestingly, Geller says that young children have no problems in bending spoons because they have not yet been taught that it is supposedly impossible.

THE MOVING SANDWICH
PK doesn't only consist of bending spoons or mending broken watches, which was another Geller phenomenon. Some PK practitioners can move objects at will. Nina Kulagina, a Russian housewife, found that she could move fountain pens and compass needles.

Another Russian woman, Nelya Mikhailova, was reputed to have made a reporter's sandwich crawl across a desk and fall off the side, purely through the power of her mind.

Uri Geller's psychic powers are still the subject of controversy over 30 years after he first became famous.

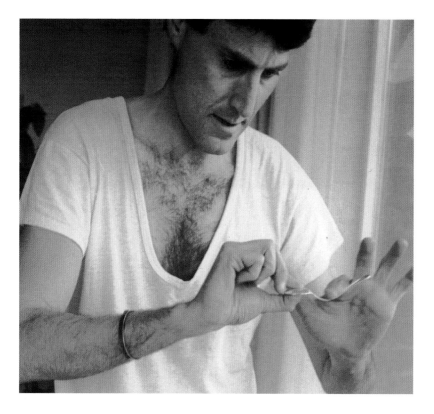

Glossary

AKASHIC RECORD An area of the astral plane that contains records of everything that has happened on Earth.

ANGEL A celestial being. The angelic kingdom is believed to be divided into three Choirs, each of which consists of three groups.

ASTRAL TRAVEL The ability to travel on the astral plane.

AURA The layer of subtle or electromagnetic energy that surrounds every living entity. The aura of humans consists of seven layers.

AUTOMATIC WRITING Writing that is produced while in communication with a spirit.

CEROMANCY A form of divination in which melted wax is tipped into a bowl of water. The shape formed by the solidified wax is then interpreted.

CHAKRA An energy point within both the aura and the human body. The seven major chakras are points at which the greatest number of energy lines within the aura converge. The four higher chakras are contained solely in the aura.

CHANNELING The ability to receive messages from a non-physical entity, often the spirit of a person who was known to the channeler.

CLAIRAUDIENT The ability to hear voices and other noises, either as an external sound or within a person's mind.

CLAIRCOGNIZANT The ability to know things without having to be told.

CLAIRSENTIENT The ability to tune into atmospheres or another person's emotional or physical sensations.

CLAIRVOYANT The ability to see spirit forms, either in the mind's eye or as a materialization.

COLLECTIVE UNCONSCIOUS
The term given by Carl Jung to a very deep level of the psyche that is shared by everyone.

CRYSTALS Precious or semi-precious stones that have powerful energetic properties. They are particularly effective when used for healing.

CRYSTAL BALL A round ball that is used for scrying. Its reflective surface can encourage the scryer to enter into a light trance.

DÉJÀ VU The sensation of repeating an event that has already taken place, even though it is actually being experienced for the first time.

DOWSING The ability to tune into the energy of a particular object using divining rods, a pendulum or the chakras in the hands.

ECTOPLASM The silky substance secreted from the body of a physical medium while in trance. The ectoplasm often builds up into the form of a spirit.

ESP Extrasensory perception, or the ability to perceive something without using any of the normal five senses.

FLOWER REMEDY A liquid made by steeping a flower in water. The resulting energized remedy brings harmony to the emotions.

GHOST A spirit form that regularly haunts a particular place. Ghosts are often the spirits of people who are unaware that they have died.

GROUNDING An essential process in psychic work which anchors a person's energy to the earth beneath him.

GUARDIAN ANGEL An angel which is assigned the role of guardian to a person throughout each of her lives and in the between-life states as well.

I CHING A Chinese method of divination which, at its highest, is considered to be a form of philosophy.

KIRLIAN PHOTOGRAPHY
A method of photographing the aura of living entities.

LUCID DREAMING The ability of a dreamer to realize that he is dreaming and to influence the outcome of his dream.

MANDALA A symbolic design and a sacred image that is often used as a focus for meditation or contemplation. In Jungian psychology it is a symbol of the self.

MASTER SPIRIT Also known as an ascended master, this is a great teacher or prophet who once lived on earth.

MEDITATION A form of contemplation or thought control in which the mind is directed inwards.

MEDIUM Also known as a sensitive, a medium is the intermediary between a living person and a spirit.

MERIDIAN One of the narrow channels which transmit energy, or *ch'i*, around the body. Meridians are particularly important in acupuncture.

NDE A near-death experience, in which a person's spirit leaves his body and travels towards, or through, a dark tunnel that leads to a source of light. At some point, the spirit returns to the body.

OOBE An out-of-body experience, in which a person's astral body briefly separates from his physical body.

PENDULUM A device, made from crystal, wood or metal, which is used for dowsing.

POLTERGEIST A disruptive spirit that moves objects or creates a noise.

PRECOGNITION The ability to know something, through psychic means, before it happens.

PREMONITION A prior warning about something which is received through psychic means.

PSYCHIC SURGERY A physical operation performed on a patient by a healer who is often in a trance.

PSYCHOKINESIS The ability to influence physical objects through the power of the mind.

PSYCHOMETRY The ability to tune into the physical and emotional history of an object by touching it.

REINCARNATION The belief, shared by many of the world's religions, that we are born again after we die.

REMOTE VIEWING The ability to observe another place or person through psychic means.

RUNES A form of divination involving a set of 24 tiles, each of which is inscribed with a letter of the ancient runic alphabet.

SCRYING The practice of gazing into a shiny or reflective surface in order to produce visions or a trance.

SOUL GROUP A group of people to whom a soul belongs, and who choose to incarnate at roughly the same time.

SOULMATE Someone you know through several lifetimes, and with whom you are likely to experience a wide range of relationships.

SPIRIT GUIDE A non-physical entity that guides a soul through its many lives.

SYNCHRONICITY The term given by Carl Jung to a meaningful coincidence. He called it "an acausal connecting theory."

TAROT CARDS A set of 72 cards, consisting of the Major and Minor Arcana, which is used for divination.

TELEPATHY The ability of one person to connect with another through the power of thought.

TWIN FLAME A soul who is the other half of your own soul.

ZENER CARDS A set of 25 cards, each bearing the image of a star, square, cross, circle or wavy lines. The image on each card is sent telepathically from one person to the other.

Bibliography

Andrews, Ted, *How to Meet and Work with Spirit Guides*, Llewellyn, 2004.

Atwater, P. M. H., *Beyond the Light: Near-Death Experiences—The Full Story*, Thorsons, 1994.

Bloom, William, *Working with Angels, Fairies and Nature Spirits*, Piatkus, 1998.

Borgia, Anthony, *Life in the World Unseen*, Odhams, 1954.

Campbell, Joseph with Moyers, Bill, *The Power of Myth*, Doubleday, 1989.

Cooke, Grace, *The New Mediumship*, White Eagle Publishing Trust, 1965.

Crowley, Vivianne, *Jungian Spirituality*, Thorsons, 1998.

Davies, Dr. Brenda, *Journey of the Soul*, Hodder Mobius, 2002.

Gerber, MD, Richard, *Vibrational Medicine for the 21st Century*, Piatkus, 2000.

Graves, Tom, *The Elements of Pendulum Dowsing*, Element, 1993.

Guirdham, Arthur, *The Cathars and Reincarnation*, C. W. Daniel, 1997.

Lewis, James R. and Oliver, Evelyn Dorothy, *Angels A to Z*, Visible Ink Press, 1996.

Minns, Sue, *Soulmates*, Hodder Mobius, 2004.

Myss, Caroline, *Why People Don't Heal and How They Can*, Bantam, 1977.

Sheldrake, Rupert, *Dogs that Know When Their Owners Are Coming Home*, Arrow, 1999.

Shine, Betty, *My Life as a Medium*, Thorsons, 1996.

Stevens, Anthony, *Jung*, Oxford University Press, 1994.

Struthers, Jane, *Tell Your Own Fortune*, Kyle Cathie, 2001.

Struthers, Jane, *The Art of Tea-leaf Reading*, Godsfield Press, 2005.

Twigg, Ena with Hagy Brod, Ruth, *Medium*, Star Books, 1974.

Van Praagh, James, *Talking to Heaven*, Piatkus Books, 1998.

Virtue, Doreen, *Archangels and Ascended Masters*, Hay House, 2003.

Weeks, Nora, *The Medical Discoveries of Dr Edward Bach, Physician*, C. W. Daniel, 1997.

White, Ian, *Australian Bush Flower Essences*, Findhorn Press, 2004.

White, Ruth, *Working with Your Chakras*, Piatkus, 1993.

Index

Acknowledgements

PICTURE ACKNOWLEDGEMENTS

Special photography: © **Octopus Publishing Group Limited**/Russell Sadur.

Other photography: Alamy 331; /Ace Stock Limited 52–53; /allOver photography 317; /Bubbles Photolibrary 300–301; /Damita Delimont 153; /Mary Evans Picture Library 249, 345, 376; /nagelestock.com 245; /Alan Novelli 254. **Bridgeman Art Library**/Bonhams, UK, Phillips, The International Fine Art Auctioneers,UK 299. **Corbis UK Limited** 106, 121, 281; /Bettmann 35; /Gary Edwards/zefa 296–297; /Blasius Erlinger/zefa 290; /David Lees 61; /Hans Neleman 40; /Vittoriano Rastelli 246–247; /Roger Ressmeyer 34; /Bo Zaunders 256; /Herbery Zetti 27. **DigitalVision** 16. **Getty Images** 113, 149, 286, 372; /Jutta Klee 379; /LWA 122. **ImageSource** 22, 119, 285, 294. **Mary Evans Picture Library** 347; /Guy Lyon Playfair 130, 383; /SPR 227. **Octopus Publishing Group Limited** 48, 159, 162, 164–165, 229, 292, 318, 370; /Bob Atkins 324, 325 top, 325 bottom; /Paul Bricknell 102, 274–275; /Stephen Conroy 266; /Fraser Cunningham 9, 12, 24, 58, 83, 85, 86, 87, 90–91, 138, 139, 143, 151, 160, 358; /Robert Estall 322; /Steve Gorton 319, 320, 323, 326, 332, 334, 336; /Colin Gotts 111, 289; /Mike Hemsley at Walter Gardiner 302; /Mike Hemsley 107, 222, 241; /Ruth Jenkinson 19, 128, 148; /Ray Moller 321; /Ian Parsons 114, 212–217; /Mike Prior 18, 65, 99, 158, 161, 167, 175, 231, 236, 258, 342; /Peter Pugh-Cook 173; /William Reavell 54, 57, 354; /Tim Ridley 327; /Ian Wallace 115; /Mark Winwood 135, 361. **PhotoDisc** 221, 233, 234, 381. **Photolibrary Group** 17, 328; /Teo Lannie 123. **Science Photo Library**/Oscar Burriel 15; /Ian Hooton 172; /Manfred Kage 13; /National Library of Medicine 47; /Alfred Pasieka 62. **TopFoto**/Charles Walker 132.

AUTHOR ACKNOWLEDGEMENTS

Many people have helped me to write this book and I should like to extend my grateful thanks to all of them. First of all, I would like to thank everyone at Godsfield Press, who have once again been great to work with. In particular, thanks to Sandra Rigby for asking me to write the book; to Jennifer Barr for being so helpful throughout; to Clare Churly for her day-to-day management of the book; and, last but by no means least, to Mandy Greenfield for her meticulous copy-editing. Thanks to my dear friend and colleague, Frank Clifford, for lending me reference books. I would also like to thank the staff at Tenderden Library, who ordered so many books on my behalf and were unfailingly helpful. As ever, my thanks and love go to my agent, Chelsey Fox, and my husband, Bill Martin. And, finally, I should like to thank Sophie and Hector, who have taught me so much.

Executive Editor Sandra Rigby
Managing Editor Clare Churly
Executive Art Editor Sally Bond
Designer Julie Francis
Picture Librarian Sophie Delpech
Production Controller Simone Nauerth